THE AMERICAN POLITICAL NOVEL

THE AMERICAN POLITICAL NOVEL

By Gordon Milne

UNIVERSITY OF OKLAHOMA PRESS

NORMAN

BY GORDON MILNE

George William Curtis and the Genteel Tradition
(Bloomington, Indiana, 1956)
The American Political Novel
(Norman, 1966)

4 ⁹⁵

22504

8/26/66

LIBRARY OF CONGRESS CATALOG CARD NUMBER: 66–13417

Copyright 1966 by the University of Oklahoma Press, Publishing Division of the University. Composed and printed at Norman, Oklahoma, U.S.A., by the University of Oklahoma Press. First edition.

*This book is affectionately dedicated
to the Arneson family*

☆

Preface

ATTRACTED to the subject of politics in literature by my reading of some Gilded Age anticorruption novels, most notably George William Curtis's *Trumps* and John De Forest's *Honest John Vane* and *Playing the Mischief*, I quickly came to agree with the astute Stendhalian comment that "politics in a work of literature is like a pistol-shot in the middle of a concert, something loud and vulgar, and yet a thing to which it is not possible to refuse one's attention." Quite willing to grant my attention, I went on to delve more deeply into the topic, becoming intrigued by the diverse political points of view of the writers of this type of fiction, astonished by their emotion-laden tones, and interested in their bringing into focus such political types as the "boss."

Questions began to arise in my mind. Did the novelists achieve their almost universally shared objective of reform? Did they avoid the exaggeration and distortion that so often mar the purpose novel? What form did they choose, satire, allegory, romance, the *roman à clef*? Were they successful in relieving the common American image of politics as sordid and venal? Did they make rational assessments of political movements like Populism or socialism?

As I decided to write an account of the American political novel, still other questions came to the fore. To what degree could a political study offer comment on the larger problems of mankind? Did political fiction give further evidence of the disappearance of the American dream? Could the career of a politician shed light on the psychology of power?

To some of the questions, at least, the answers came— and they seemed worth sharing with others. Knowing that politics has always aroused the American people (indeed, in these days of mass communication media, it seems to absorb them more than ever), I assumed that my answers—even the unanswered questions—might persuade a number of individuals not to "refuse attention." I therefore proceeded with the book, hoping to draw to the subject not just the political scientist, the historian, and the student of literature, but the general reader as well.

Critics have examined the form before, of course, Morris Speare having written the pioneer work, *The Political Novel, Its Development in England and America,* in 1924. However, Speare's book lays much more stress on the development of the English version than on that of the American, simply nodding in the direction of writers such as Henry Adams and Winston Churchill, and leaving much room for expansion. His successors have been few, and they, too, have left gaps. Joseph Blotner's essay *The Political Novel,* though very stimulating, functions primarily, as the author himself says, as a teaching aid for the political science instructor. Irving Howe's *Politics and the Novel* is a most intelligent book, as one might expect, but highly selective and thus not a "study" of the genre. Certain unpublished doctoral dissertations have dealt with the topic—Jean Johnson's *The American Political Novel in the Nineteenth Century* the most satisfactorily— but have not attempted to be inclusive, nor especially critical.

Thus, the way appears open for another examination of the type. I have tried to lend thoroughness to mine by establishing a sufficiently comprehensive chronological pattern, but I have also tried to pursue a constantly analytical course. If my treatment has proved successful, it should adequately suggest the nature and the merits of this lively fictional form and should also serve as another indication of the inevitable link between literature and "society," in this case, the "body politic."

GORDON MILNE

December, 1965
Lake Forest, Illinois

Contents

THE AMERICAN POLITICAL NOVEL

☆

CHAPTER I

Introduction

WHEN one focuses his attention on that intriguing but rather rarely discussed topic the American political novel, one quickly discovers that the old axiom "nothing new under the sun" applies. The form has a history, and indeed quite a long one. It was not new when Allen Drury's *Advise and Consent* recently caught the public fancy; it was not new in the 1900's when muckraking was in style, nor even in the post–Civil War "exposure" era.

The genre seems to go back to the early nineteenth century, when the political allegories and political satires of these and of preceding years began turning into a form truly resembling the novel. At almost the same moment the type caught on in England, and it spread to the Continent as well.[1] In this country it could not be called a thriving genre until the 1870's, but thereafter an increasing number of such pieces of fiction appeared, culminating in the 1900–10 "progressive period" boom, when countless novels came tumbling forth.[2] Its popularity, world-wide, has continued in the

[1] One thinks of Disraeli, Trollope, Eliot, Meredith, Conrad, Dostoevski, and Stendhal. Irving Howe calls Dostoevski's *The Possessed* the greatest of all political novels. See Irving Howe, *Politics and the Novel*, 22.

[2] Forty-seven novels in that decade alone, according to William B. Dickens. See William B. Dickens, "A Guide to the American Political Novel, 1865–1910," unpublished Ph.D. dissertation, University of Michigan, 1953, i.

3

twentieth century, the work of Silone, Koestler, Malraux, Orwell, and of, for the most part, "lesser" Americans having attracted many readers in these more recent times.

The genre has been variously defined. Morris Speare, the first to offer a substantial discussion of the subject, calls it:

> . . . a work of prose fiction which leans rather to 'ideas' than to 'emotions'; which deals rather with the machinery of law-making or with a theory about public conduct than with the merits of any given piece of legislation; and where the main purpose of the writer is party propaganda, public reform, or exposition of the lives of the personages who maintain government, or of the forces which constitute government. In this exposition the drawing-room is frequently used as a medium for presenting the inside life of politics.[3]

H. A. L. Fisher confines himself to saying that the political novel concerns itself with men and women engaged in contemporary political life and discussing contemporary political ideas,[4] and William B. Dickens accepts this definition, with the elimination of the word "contemporary."[5] Joseph Blotner designates the type as "a book which directly describes, interprets or analyzes political phenomena,"[6] whereas Irving Howe declares it to be one in which political ideas play a dominant role or in which the political milieu is the dominant setting.[7] Mrs. Jean O. Johnson seems to prefer

[3] Morris E. Speare, *The Political Novel, Its Development in England and America*, ix.
[4] H. A. L. Fisher, "The Political Novel," *Cornhill Magazine*, n.s., vol. 64 (January, 1928), 27.
[5] Dickens, *op. cit.*, 3.
[6] Joseph L. Blotner, *The Political Novel*, 2.   [7] Howe, *op. cit.*, 17.

4

another description by Howe: the political novelist's subject "is the relation between politics and literature, and . . . the term 'political novel' is used . . . as a convenient shorthand to suggest the kind of novel in which this relation is interesting enough to warrant investigation."[8]

According to these interpretations, the essentials of political fiction would seem to be the presence of political ideas and of the political milieu. One might include in the genre, let us say, novels illustrating a conflict between two ideologies such as Communism and democracy, or novels examining the connection between the political figure and the body politic, indicating the degree to which he is independent of and yet a part of this body. One may also demonstrably include fiction with the political scene as background and books which offer accounts of politicians and political careers.

The problem of definition is somewhat compounded by the close relationship among political, economic, and social novels, and between the political novel and such a specialized form as "utopian" fiction. Mrs. Johnson's warning— "Efforts to create rigid classifications to distinguish the political novel from the economic, the social, the proletarian, and other related types are likely not only to be unsuccessful but to detract from an understanding of the development of the novel rather than to add to it"[9]—is sensible, and I have chosen to follow her pattern of avoiding very inflexible stratification. Therefore, my discussion would not necessarily eschew a primarily economic work like *The Jungle* or a pri-

8 *Ibid.* Quoted in Jean O. Johnson, "The American Political Novel in the Nineteenth Century," unpublished Ph.D. dissertation, Boston University, 1958, p. 1.
9 Johnson, *op. cit.*, 4.

marily utopian piece like *Looking Backward*; at the same time it generally steers clear of the economic, social protest, proletarian, and utopian areas, areas which have already received the careful attention of such scholars as Walter Taylor, Vernon Parrington, Jr., and Walter Rideout.

In the course of our study we shall make suggestions as to the impact of the political novel upon society (though this intricate question is not easily resolved), and as to the purely "literary" worth of this type of fiction. Since "exposure literature" obviously tends toward the didactic and polemical, it runs the severe risk of being inartistic. Many political novels *are* inartistic, structurally discursive, rhetorical in tone, too manipulative of plot and character to fit the thesis, and stylistically pedestrian ("long passages of didactic exposition often alternate with sticky sentiment").[10] But the best fiction of this type does possess aesthetic worth. It offers a significant theme and one which is worked out to a denouement resulting from a logical development of characters and plot, it presents lifelike and in some cases memorable characters, and it is couched in a competent style.

Whether aesthetically pleasing or not, political novels usually make fascinating reading—probably for the simple reason that "politics rakes our passions as nothing else."[11] Although most Americans no longer hang around the cracker barrel in the village store, they go on discussing political issues and political candidates with considerable avidity. They talk, they watch the national conventions on TV, *and* they read; witness the tremendous success of *Advise and Consent*.

[10] *Ibid.*, 318.
[11] Howe, *op. cit.*, 24.

6

Introduction

Just as a political discussion is apt to be heated, so is a political novel. The best ones, well, even the worst, generate considerable passion, bringing their ideas to life, stirring the reader's emotions,[12] and provoking controversy. If, for example, one reads Ruth Chatterton's attack on McCarthyism (*The Betrayers*, 1953), he feels the flames of passion rising within him over the issue, an issue supposedly quite moribund at the present time. Or, if one reads Edwin O'Connor's essentially sympathetic portrayal of the boss system (*The Last Hurrah*, 1956), he finds himself endorsing it heartily or else disapproving enthusiastically. In either case, he gets excited!

Our account of the American political novel tradition will follow a chronological pattern, with the historical background of the successive periods sketched in lightly, as the pattern unfolds.[13] Instead of attempting to deal with each or even most of the vast horde of political novels which have been produced, we shall discuss generally the ingredients of this fiction, the targets attacked, the stand of the author, the strengths and weaknesses of the form, and thus its essential value. A handful of the better novels will be singled out for

[12] I cannot agree with Morris Speare's statement, quoted on page 2, that political fiction leans rather to ideas than to emotions. In the political novel they tend to be inseparable. As Louis Rubin reminds us, if the political scientist abstracts, the political novelist concretizes, that is, dramatizes the ideas as he puts them in terms of personal experience. See Louis D. Rubin, Jr., "Politics and the Novel," address before the American Political Science Association, September 8, 1961.

[13] The historical framework must, to some degree, be supplied since the majority of political novels, based as they are on current affairs, demand some knowledge of the history of their time. As neither an historian nor a political scientist, I do not pretend to extensive knowledge of this framework but trust that the background material supplied is accurate in outline.

7

special attention, with the conviction planted in the reader's mind, we trust, that these, at least, deserve a permanent place in American literature. The *good* "opinion novels" contain drama as well as propaganda, and their treatise is subtly presented. Even if the reader refuses to accept the thesis, he feels his own commitments complicated and is altered and even "enriched" by the work—perhaps to the point of moving into the political arena himself. The political novelist would like that.

☆

CHAPTER II

The Attack Is Mounted (1774-1865)

JUST as political concerns occupied many Americans in the era from the Revolutionary War to the Civil War, so political affairs engaged the attention of American writers in that period. Some of the first attempts at fiction glanced at man as a political animal, and their successors (e.g., *Uncle Tom's Cabin*) reflected the political debates of the times. A surprising number of novelists were bent on approaching "the dark and bloody crossroads where literature and politics meet."[1]

In making this approach, writers invariably chose to present the political scene of their own era, thus discussing first the problems of governmental organization which beset the founding fathers, then such early nineteenth century issues as the juridical system, the national bank, Indian affairs, and the African slave trade. Their treatment of these questions was, from the beginning, perfectly forthright, and as a consequence the literature-politics crossroads were truly to seem at times "dark and bloody."

Even in the earliest days of its existence our new democracy did not escape unscathed, the question of States' rights coming immediately into the picture, and controversy springing up directly about such combustible matters as the whisky

[1] Lionel Trilling, *The Liberal Imagination*, 11.

tax and various sectional differences. Both the post-Revolutionary pamphlet and newspaper warfare between Republicans and Federalists and later that between Jacksonian Democrats and Whigs found echoes in the fiction of the age. Late eighteenth century political allegorists, Francis Hopkinson (*A Pretty Story*, 1774) and Jeremy Belknap (*The Foresters*, 1792), for example, demonstrated Federalist sympathies, as did also the creator of the first indisputably political novel, Hugh Henry Brackenridge (*Modern Chivalry*, 1792–1815). These writers, particularly Brackenridge, struck a note that was to be frequently sounded in the early nineteenth century, suspicion of the tyranny of the majority and a desire to educate the public so that they would perform properly as voters in a democracy.

It is actually a bit difficult to declare precisely what political ideology is endorsed in these early fictions. Brackenridge was, in fact, a Republican, yet he manages to denounce both Jeffersonian *and* Hamiltonian doctrines in the course of writing *Modern Chivalry* (the many volumes of which were published at intervals over several years). Most of his energy is devoted to attacking the already ingrained American habit of electing unqualified men (Traddles the weaver) to public office—a worthy target, even if it stemmed from the author's "sour grapes" at his own political disappointments. As a lawyer and judge he supported the role of the courts and of the law and evidenced marked concern at the despotism of mob action which sometimes, as in the Whisky Insurrection, took the law into its own hands. His position is essentially conservative, his most fervent wish for America being a ruling class of educated men.

Although scattering his fire too broadly (his targets are manifold, yellow journalism, social hypocrisy, scientific pretension, and many others appearing side by side with the political objects of attack), and though failing to present clear-cut political theories, Brackenridge does provide his fellow citizens with the first opportunity they had had to "observe themselves and their new government in the pages of fiction."[2]

In the 1830's and 1840's, writers, mostly taking their cue from Brackenridge, began protesting against the presence in public office of selfish politicos, who manipulated the masses for their own ends rather than for the good of the country. This, they felt, was what "coonskin Jacksonianism" had brought. John Pendleton Kennedy's *Quodlibet* (1840), for example, attacks the Democrats' propensity to encourage the assumption of political power by the common man and shows a preference for putting control in the hands of the aristocratic merchant class. As a supporter of Henry Clay and an unabashed Whig, Kennedy frankly asserts that the rising industrial leaders should handle the affairs of the nation.

While others take a similar antidemocratic tack, James K. Paulding holds firm to the agrarianism of Thomas Jefferson and to the latter's faith in true equality and thus supports the position of the Jacksonian Democrats. The incidental comments on political matters in his books *Koningsmarke* (1823) and *Westward Ho* (1832) reflect his insistence on the plain man in politics and on the need for social and civic equality.

Although few of the novelists so far mentioned concen-

[2] Johnson, *op. cit.*, 59.

trate exclusively on politics in their literary productions, yet even passing reference to affairs of this nature gives their books a special flavor and some added interest. One is reminded of Stendhal's comment that "politics in a work of literature is like a pistol-shot in the middle of a concert, something loud and vulgar, and yet a thing to which it is not possible to refuse one's attention."[3] American novelists, as they turn to political themes (discussing governmental theories) and to political backgrounds (exposing the evils of corruption or the vulgarities of public life), begin to command attention, especially since they are apt to report in a vociferous fashion.

The most interesting among these pioneers in the area of the political novel is James Fenimore Cooper. Although still best known as the Leatherstocking romancer, Cooper, we should bear in mind, produced a considerable body of fiction involving social, political, and even economic criticism, and his tales, amidst the loving descriptions of the north woods and the high seas, hint of the political turbulence of the "age of Jackson." If he did not sit down to write a book about the political boss or about "inside Washington," yet he sprinkled throughout his adventure plots commentary on the efficacy of various political systems and on current political "goings-on."

In his "political" novels Cooper indulged in a double-edged attack, on European government on the one hand, on American government on the other. He thoroughly disliked the feudal society of the former, with its class distinc-

[3] Quoted in Howe, *op. cit.*, 15.

tions and sharp sense of a social hierarchy; his novels *The Headsman* (1833) and *The Bravo* (1831), for example, picture Swiss and Venetian "republics," which are not true republics at all. On the other hand, he mistrusted the demagogic spirit of American democracy, especially as it operated in the Jacksonian era. Although approving of the constitutional framework of the American government, with its system of checks and balances and tripartite division, he found the system, in actual practice, to be not without flaw—in fact, sometimes, as Cooper gruffly put it, "the quintessence of hocus-pocus."

His principal objection was not registered against the constitutional setup, but rather against the strong emphasis stemming from it on the absolute power of the majority's will. The majority, so often demagogue-led, can be irrational and fractious and quite in the wrong on various issues. In truth, there is nothing more disastrous, so Cooper felt, than the leveling tendency of "mobocracy." The mass is perverted by the power of money and by the will of unscrupulous politicians and journalists. Public opinion, herdlike, merely echoes the insincere speeches of the former and the distorted accounts of the latter.

Echoing John Adams, Cooper proclaimed that an aristocracy of talent was needed, with the power to lead placed in the hands of this "minority." Men with intellect, education, and breeding should "represent" the people, looking out for their interests, helping to educate them, and so on. Such an aristocratic-led group is wise, not self-seeking nor humbugging, nor demagogic (like Aristabulus Bragg in

Home As Found). It regards political power as a public trust, granted by the constituent to the representative and properly wielded by him.

These leaders—in Cooper's somewhat archaic scheme of things—were to be drawn from the landowner class, the agrarian squirearchy of old New York patroons, *not* from the rising capitalistic order, the Wall Street exploiters, chasing busily after what Washington Irving called at this time the "Almighty Dollar." Men "to the manor born" were the ones to prevent the bumptious leveling process of a coonskin democracy.

Because of his peculiar sympathy for the "men of property" group, Cooper was much agitated when the antirent wars were precipitated in the state of New York in the early 1840's. This movement, to break up the huge landed estates and to distribute property more equally, offended Cooper, who was himself one of the"squires." He devoted a trilogy of novels to the subject, *Satanstoe* (1845), *The Chainbearer* (1845), and *The Redskins* (1846), the most directly concerned with the topic being the last in the series. Believing in the justice of the property rights of the landed proprietors (it was their land, why should they be deprived of it?) and in their intelligent and benevolent treatment of their tenants, he violently opposed the antirenters. If the rent system perhaps smacked too much of the feudal, still, property rights had been guaranteed by state and national constitutions; furthermore, the violent resistance to rent collection was extralegal. Cooper questioned the motives of the antirenters—it was covetousness, not the "liberty" about which they cried so loud, the personal gain of something for nothing, not a

14

disinterested democratic socialism—criticized their methods (the marauding "Injun" band in *The Redskins*), and again emphasized the need for regarding the "majority" with suspicion and, conversely, often heeding the will of the minority.

A typical attack on the unprincipled political agitator who plays upon the unthinking majority is to be found in Cooper's *Home As Found* (1838). Here John Effingham, a landowner, notes with dismay, on his return from an extended stay in Europe, the rise to power of his land agent, Aristabulus Bragg, a clever but unscrupulous, aggressive but pushing and insensitive individual, devoid of a sense of personal pride or tradition. Bragg illustrates—and so unhappily, Cooper feels—the "new leader," one who skillfully but selfishly manipulates the not sufficiently educated masses. As Cooper says elsewhere (*The Ways of the Hour*, 1850), "the demagogue must have his war-cry as well as the Indian; and it is probable he will continue to whoop as long as the country contains minds weak enough to furnish him with dupes."

An interesting and little-known Cooper novel, *The Crater* (1848), underlines the distrust perennially felt by the author with regard to the people—the "dupes." The book, a venture into the field of utopian fiction, describes an ideal community established by the hero Mark Woolston on some islands in the South Seas. An oligarchical organization is maintained, with "Governor" Woolston and his "council" in control: Mark Woolston "was much too sensible a man to fall into any of the modern absurdities on the subject of equality, and a community of interests." The community begins to fall apart, however, when a few rabble-rousers convince the masses that they are not running and should be running their own affairs. A tyranny of the majority results, interest being substituted for principle, and public virtue becoming a frail thing indeed. The majority do not really rule anyway, but rather their irresponsible manipulators (e.g., the editor of the colony's newspaper).

An all-important political truth, Cooper declares, is "that the more a people attempt to extend their power directly over state affairs, the less they, in fact, control them, after having once passed the point of naming lawgivers as their representatives; merely bestowing on a few artful managers the influence they vainly imagine to have secured to themselves." After the "artful managers" have undermined the Woolston regime, the settlement assumes an anything-but-utopian character, as individual rights are jeopardized and disunity is everywhere in evidence. Romancer Cooper finally provides a neat solution to the dilemma thus posed, by having the islands, as the result of an earthquake, disappear into the sea. It should be added that Woolston and the other "good ones" have been conveniently removed elsewhere before retribution falls.

Another Cooper novel with political implications is *The Monikins* (1836), a Swiftian political allegory, satirizing both England and America. This novel (if it can be called such)[4] describes the visit of Sir John Goldencalf and Captain Noah Poke to the countries of Leaphigh (England), Leapthrough (France), and Leaplow (America), where monikins (monkey-men) dwell.

In "Leaphigh" the visitors are disturbed by the presence

---

[4] As a satiric allegory the book is in the tradition of Hopkinson's *A Pretty Story* and Belknap's *The Foresters*.

of inequality, of honors falling to those to whom they are least due, of courts judging on the basis of impulse rather than reason, of fawning courtiers and of the empty form and ceremony of the state religion. Nothing is pure or free from the taint of falsehood, selfishness, or vanity. In "Leaplow," on the other hand, Sir John and Captain Noah are bothered by abuses in the political system of a different sort. The sachem (president), riddles (senators), and other political people, though originally good, have grown corrupt. Faction runs rampant among the political parties, the Horizontals, Perpendiculars, and Tangents, and these groups often nominate unqualified men (the cabin boy whom they select recalls Brackenridge's Traddles the weaver or the "bog-trotter" Teague O'Regan) for office and indulge in campaigns marked by lying and chicanery. Many in the electorate are not qualified for voting privileges, and pecuniary interest motivates most of those who *are*. Moral principle disappears before material concern. Sir John's conclusions are gloomy: every man loves liberty for *his* own sake; moral saltation is necessary to political success; hypocrisy is the most flourishing 'ocracy; all our wisdom is insufficient to protect us from frauds; men have more of the habits, propensities, cravings, and antics of "monikins" than is generally or willingly admitted.

Much of Cooper's criticism of political affairs has a valid air about it. His "times" were marked by the selfishness and fraudulence—we recall the introduction of the spoils system, the flourishing of parties such as the Locofocos, the Hunkers, and the Know-Nothings—on which he so emphatically commented. Although his peculiar bias toward oligarchical control in governmental matters does not win wholehearted endorsement, the modern reader being no more ready to accept the Dutch patroon as leader than Cooper was the "captain of industry," his free-swinging (a very testy man was Fenimore Cooper) remarks on the body politic generally have the ring of truth.

In the work of Cooper a prevailing pattern for the nineteenth century American political novel begins to be discernible. Primarily *un*concerned with discussing political ideologies, it focuses instead on describing the political scene and its actors, finding evidence of ugliness and corruption in the former, dishonesty and brainlessness among the latter. Adopting a lofty "gentleman's view" it looks on at "the melee from the bleachers with . . . disgust."[5]

Among those who joined Cooper in watching scornfully from the bleachers were writers such as N. B. Tucker and Frederick Thomas. Tucker's *The Partisan Leader* (1836) offers as a cure for factionalism a peculiarly Southern panacea, the preservation of the plantation system and the vesting of governmental power in the hands of the aristocracy. Thomas calls for the presence in public life of the "preux chevalier" type, too, though, as a Northerner, he would probably not limit his "acceptable" list to the Southern planter group. Thomas's *Clinton Bradshaw* (1835) outlines the career of an honest lawyer, who reaches the Congressional halls despite having to climb a ladder festooned with vilification and deceit. In several respects this novel indicates the "shape

[5] Johnson, *op. cit.*, 3. Mrs. Johnson, remarking on the detachment of this view, points out that the gentleman had been rather roughly "shoved outside the political arena by Jacksonian democracy and big business alike."

of things to come" in political fiction: its political maneuvering subject matter, its lawyer-protagonist, its biographical structure, and its subsidiary sentimental love story. The nineteenth century political novel is apt to be a political romance!

Probably the most "informed" example of political fiction in the pre-Civil War period is George William Curtis's *Trumps* (1861). The work of a man who was already a political pundit, and who was to become an influential Republican party leader and even a President-maker, the novel provides an authentic glimpse of American "politicking" on city, state, and national levels. In particular, it casts aspersions on New York's Tammany Hall, an organization which had been merrily grafting its way since the 1820's and which had received especially unfavorable publicity in the 1850's during the regime of Fernando Wood and his "council of the forty thieves."

Although primarily intent upon telling a love story (in fact, several love stories), *Trumps* contains many discussions of political affairs, with Curtis briskly bombarding such evils as vicious legislation, dishonest campaigns, and an unqualified electorate, and giving an unvarnished account of the workings of a political machine such as Tammany's. Behind his knowledgeable presentation of unsavory political activity lies a strong plea for "good government."

The subplot of *Trumps* provides the political commentary. Focusing on Abel Newt, a young-man-about-New York, it depicts his venture into the political arena. With the backing of a powerful city machine (which buys off the no longer desirable incumbent), Abel secures the nomination for Congress from his district. His motives in running for the position, Curtis emphasizes, are purely selfish. He has dissipated an inheritance and plans to recoup via politics. The field, he knows, offers countless opportunities to make money. His backers' motives prove no less selfish, for they anticipate his supporting—once he is in Congress—a bill, the passage of which will result in large financial returns to them.

With the aid of this smoothly functioning political organization, which has already fixed the nominating convention by sending to it a slate of delegates who "understand things," and which now "fixes" a sufficient number of voters, Abel wins the election. Unfortunately, by the time his election has become certain, and his "supporters" (paid off in various ways by the machine) have come to serenade the winner, Abel has already carried his private celebration so far that he is too drunk to respond to his audience. This rather bothers his managers since, according to their realistic dictum, "if a man expects to succeed in political life he must understand when not to be drunk." But they're willing to overlook one slip.

Abel does go ahead to become a successful representative, that is, one well versed in the principle of "senatorial courtesy"—you support this measure for me, and I will support that one for you. By means of a clever speech in Congress he secures the necessary votes for the passage of the bill in which his backers are interested, and he wends his way neatly through the Washington world of selfishness and intrigue. Before long, however, he succumbs to personal weaknesses, his passion for gambling and for liquor, and as a result is killed in a barroom brawl. His original supporters, after issuing high-sounding resolutions about the lamentable death of

Congressman Newt ("a friend of the people," "an enemy of the purse-proud aristocracy"), go hastily searching for another less personally weak and equally tractable tool.

In treating Abel Newt and his confreres, Curtis shows considerable candor. The will of the people, he makes clear, is subservient to the self-interest of party leaders. The public is an ass, says one official—"only," he adds in warning, "never let it think so." The voters act like so many sheep in their gregarious and stupid following of the professional politicians. Political control rests firmly in the hands of "bosses" such as General Arcularius Belch, who, from his shabby law office, quietly dictates the party line. Recognizing the need for constant discipline and a steady hand on the crank, the General keeps the machinery operating smoothly, bending to his will both the Honorable B. T. Ele, congressman, and the shyster lawyer, Aquila Bat, both Enos Slugby, chairman of the ward committee, and the district leaders—large, coarse-featured, hulking men . . . all named Jim, or Tom, or Ned."

With the knowledge that "life is a scrub-race," in which the devil takes the hindmost, Belch keeps his eye on the main chance and "grabs for gold" at every opportunity. Not at all concerned with the need for the enactment of good laws or the encouragement of unselfish public service, he puts into office men like Abel Newt, who are completely self-centered, worldly, and unsqueamish ("I do respect a man who has no scruples," says the General), and he makes no attempt to secure benefits for the voters.

Without exception the politicians in *Trumps* belong to a lower order of being, whether they function in the top political echelon like Representative Condor, in the middle like Alderman O'Rourke, or on the bottom like district boss Slugby. No "gentleman," the author remarks, knows anything of the running of the government. Abel Newt (a gentleman, if on the black sheep order) entered politics only to improve his reduced circumstances; others conveniently ignore the subject and would not dream of participating in the political hurly-burly. This is Curtis's chief cause for complaint. The "better" men, he insists, must interest themselves in the affairs of the nation in order that the government may improve. They cannot simply view "the melee from the bleachers with disgust."

If a forceful indictment of political evils, *Trumps* is vitiated by several technical weaknesses. The main and subplots do not easily cohere; the cast includes—with the exception of Abel Newt—a series of stock characters; sentimentality and melodrama (the barroom brawl) play too large a role; and the irony (those supposedly funny proper names, Belch, Bat, Slugby, Condor) is ponderous. Although Curtis has a capable style and a command of his subject, he lacks the depth and finish which would bestow subtlety and weight upon his novel. *Trumps*—there is no denying—has a "dated" air.

The same may be said for most of its predecessors in the pre-Civil War period.[6] These early political novels are better social documents than literature, their authors being, as a

---

[6] There have been several historical novels, written at a considerably later date, about the politics of this period. Irving Bacheller's *The Light in the Clearing* (1917), for example, deals with the career of Silas Wright, governor of New York in the 1840's. See A. T. Dickinson, Jr., *American Historical Fiction*, 38.

rule, too angry to consider craftsmanship. They interest us, however, in their indication of the warping of American political ideals, and in their setting up of the "targets" at which more and more writers will fire in the latter half of the century.

☆

CHAPTER III

The Spirit of Protest (1865–1900)

POLITICAL fiction flourished like the green bay tree after the Civil War, with more than forty novels of political activity appearing in the closing decades of the nineteenth century. In these works are to be found extended discussions of how political machinery—campaigns, nominating conventions, legislative sessions—operated, and of what politicians were like. Their writers sought—most earnestly—to make the voter, John Q. Public, "aware" of corruption and malfeasance in political circles and to convince him that proper government was largely his responsibility. The spirit of protest was abroad in the land.

Even the most superficial survey of the history of the post-Civil War era reveals very readily the need for public "awareness." As its most familiar sobriquet "the Gilded Age" informs us, it was a time when materialism ran rampant, when the gospel of wealth was heartily worshipped, when captains of industry (less flatteringly, "robber barons" or "moguls") came to the fore. Most important for the political novelist, it was an age when the newly established "big business" allied itself with the American government. The alliance was usually made for selfish purposes, the huge corporations exerting unremitting pressure on all branches of government to further their own ends. Sometimes by persuasion, more often by economic pressure, intimidation, or even outright bribery, the railways and public utility companies dominated city councils, state legislatures, even Congress and the courts, securing advantageous land grants, franchises, and favors of many kinds.

As this condition suggests, it was an age of guilt as well as gilt, an era of "boodle," of "Get It," of open and shameless corruption in public life. Scandals by the dozen marred the postwar years. In the cynical seventies came an exposé of the Tweed Ring, controlling from Tammany Hall and coining money by the wholesale graft system. Boss William Marcy Tweed proved to be in league with the mayor of New York Oakey Hall (called "O. K. Haul" by political cartoonist Thomas B. Nast) in bribing legislative bodies, and the size of their swindles was Himalayan. Significantly, Tammany recovered quickly from the exposure, and by the mid-eighties was blithely pursuing, under Boss "I-am-working-for-my-pockets-all-the-time" Richard Croker, its old ways.[1] The reform agitation which cropped up again in 1892, when police participation in vote frauds was discovered, proved hardly more permanent.

Also in the 1870's the *Crédit Mobilier* scandal came to light, an affair involving such influential government officials as Representative James A. Garfield and Vice-President Schuyler Colfax. The Whisky Ring, operating from 1870 on

[1] An example of Croker's method of proceeding: announcing that a state supreme court justice, Joseph F. Daly, veteran of twenty-eight years of service on the bench, would not be renominated, he said, "We had a a right to expect proper consideration from Judge Daly who owed his nomination and election to Tammany Hall. We didn't get it. That's why we turned him down.' Quoted in J. Rogers Hollingsworth, *The Whirligig of Politics*, 142.

25

and defrauding the government of millions of dollars in taxes, was uncovered in 1875, and again governmental officials were involved, this time Orville Babcock, President Grant's private secretary. These and numerous other shady imbroglios —the Star Route and Indian frauds—clouded Grant's basically disreputable administrations. The disturbing thing—at least to the political novelists—was that government officers appeared to be such easy corruptees and that public opinion remained largely indifferent, or even condoned the *status quo*. When, for example, Congressman Oakes Ames' role in the *Crédit Mobilier* affair, the dissemination to various political figures of free shares in a Union Pacific construction company, was exposed, no public hostility was shown him. The era of the "smooth deal," of influence peddlers and 5 per centers had already arrived.

It was, in fact, as Henry Adams remarked, an *ordinary* period, in American politics,[2] a time when the destinies of the nation were controlled by "average" men such as Ulysses S. Grant, James G. Blaine, and Roscoe Conkling, "leaders" who were more interested in exploiting the nation's resources than in protecting them, more interested in their own welfare than in the nation's. As such, they permitted lavish subsidies, charter grants and high tariffs, and were themselves often personally interested as stockholders or lawyers in corporate enterprises which might be affected by their votes as legislators. They were spoilsmen for the most part, too, un-

[2] H. Wayne Morgan holds an opposing view—"Few generations produced a more striking set of party leaders, contrary to the views of many scholars who portray it as an age of drab issues and dull men"—but offers relatively little evidence in support of his position. See H. Wayne Morgan (ed.), *The Gilded Age: A Reappraisal*, 6.

interested in civil service reform and, in fact, delaying it for many years. They could not imagine the motives of the reformers—there must be a "gimmick." A "single-minded concern for honesty in public service is a luxury,"[3]—thus, their cynical attitude.

Such was the politician in the 1870–1900 period, cynical, corruptible. The congressman used his influence illegally in land speculation and mining schemes. The state legislator heeded the "requests" of railroad and manufacturing interests. The city official bowed down before the political boss. In city government, indeed, conditions were the worst of all. The machine system operated in most of the large cities, bosses controlling, and under them a highly organized political setup, stretching through the ward-heelers to the voters. Tool candidates were put up for office, votes were bought recklessly, even the would-be reformers often succumbed to the financial lure of the machine. For such conditions the unaware *or* apathetic public must, concluded the political novelists, take the blame.

The question arises, *were* the people aware of the abysses beneath the smiling surface of the Gilded Age? Did they know that beneath skyrocketing industry and the resulting substantial financial profit for a few lay such evils as stock-watering and bogus dividends? Did they recognize the sharper class distinctions coming in the wake of the rising plutocracy? Did they see the social problems involved in the increase in immigration and the growth of cities?

Some critics have answered these questions in the negative. Grant Knight, for one, said of the era:

[3] Richard Hofstadter, *The American Political Tradition,* 175.

27

. . . one of the strangest in our history: ostensibly dedicated to all the virtues, yet practicing few; an age which mingled public idealism with private rapacity; people being as unconscious of wrong-doing, seemingly, as the individuals of the Renaissance who left religious meditations or services to murder their rivals.[4]

But Knight's opinion was counteracted by many, e.g., Edward Cassady[5] and Wayne Morgan, the latter forthrightly declaring that "public interest in government was very much alive. . . . Few periods have had so articulate a set of reformers with so many organs open to them for disseminating their views. . . . There is no evidence, furthermore, that the public was more tolerant of corruption than before or after the Gilded Age."[6]

And so it would seem as one reads both the histories and the literature of the period. Numerous humanitarian-minded individuals were agitating for various reforms in the seventies and eighties and nineties, for legislation to regulate working hours and working conditions and to control the railroads and trusts (n.b., the Sherman Antitrust Act of 1890), and some concerned souls were attempting to recapture for the people the agencies of government and to "purify" politics. The third-party movements—Grangers, Greenbackers, Knights of Labor, Populists—give evidence of this, as do the corrective schemes of reformers like Henry George and Edward Bellamy, the tartly-worded articles in magazines such as the *Atlantic Monthly* and *North American Review*, the *Nation*

[4] Grant C. Knight, *American Literature and Culture*, 288.
[5] Edward E. Cassady, "Muckraking in the Gilded Age," *American Literature*, Vol. 13 (May, 1941), 135–41.
[6] Morgan, *op. cit.*, 6, 9.

and *Harper's,* and the many novels of social protest which were published in these decades. If the muckraking era still remained ahead, yet the note of agitation sounded and re-sounded in the "wasteland of Grant" and thereafter, and much writing that was partisanly directed not only to inform but also to *reform* was freely circulating in the postwar era.

A frequently chosen vehicle for the expression of protest was the political novel. If the protest proceeded along various lines—utopian (Bellamy's *Looking Backward,* Ignatius Don-nelly's *Caesar's Column*), economic (Elizabeth Phelps' *The Silent Partner*), economic-political (Henry Keenan's *The Moneymakers,* David R. Locke's *A Paper City,* Rebecca Harding Davis's *John Andross*)—the political implications of the fiction were always apparent, e.g., the description of fin-anciers indicating their exertion of political pressure, or the discussion of class conflict leading to the conclusion that government remained in the hands of the well-heeled rather than in those of the masses.

Surveying the political horizon, the novelists quickly singled out certain targets for attack, maintaining a heavy fire throughout the period on governmental abuses. The spoils system aroused the ire of many, the wholesale turnover of personnel at the end of each national administration (at least, when the party in power changed) seeming a tremen-dous waste, and the practice of handing out political ap-pointments promiscuously seeming a deleterious one. In *Through One Administration* (1881) Frances Hodgson Bur-nett mourns the sudden loss of a job for no good reason and indirectly attacks the patronage system. F. Marion Crawford comes to her support in *An American Politician* (1884), in which the leading figure, honest (and unbearably dull) John Harrington pleads for civil service reform. A contrast is offered by the character of Caleb Mason in David R. Locke's *The Demagogue* (1891), who knows how to stay in power by means of the spoils system, keeping loyal henchman in key spots, from the local post office up to more strategic billets.

Much criticism was also brought to bear on the widespread abuse of lobbying, the presence in Washington and in state capitals of pressure groups working on the legislators for selfish ends. The Amorys in Mrs. Burnett's book, for example, are trying to maneuver a Westoria lands arrangement, indulging in "wheeler-dealer" operations in the process. Laura Hawkins in Mark Twain and Charles Dudley Warner's *The Gilded Age* (1873) provides another illustration. Laura is engaged in lobbying for the Knobs University bill, a scheme to found an industrial school for freed Negroes. Behind this seemingly innocent and altruistic design, lies a desire to sell, at an exorbitant price, land belonging to the Hawkins family, on which to establish the school. The idea of the school is really no more than a blind. Working hand in glove with the corrupt Senator Dilworthy, Laura secures the support of various key political figures, using a little blackmail and relying on the "senatorial courtesy" principle. As always, it is money that makes the mare go.

A less well-known target for the political novelist was the power of the corporation. Even in this fairly early stage of the consolidation process in business, the big bogey of the corporation's rule was recognized by a few. Rebecca Harding Davis saw the power which it exerted over state if not national legislatures, and in *John Andross* (1874) pilloried a railroad corporation which, having "tools" in the Pennsylvania legislature, used them as bribing instruments to secure votes on essential bills. Hamlin Garland described the same pattern in *A Spoil of Office* (1892). In this novel corporations control the Iowa legislature, as the young congressman hero discovers to his dismay. In another book of Garland's, *A Member of the Third House* (1892), a railroad corporation legislative stranglehold is at length broken.

Legislative bodies themselves come in for a fair share of criticism. The members, as has been shown, allow themselves to be tempted by big business. They look out for themselves first, says Garland, the corporation second, and the public third. Having no conscience where public money is concerned, they appropriate lavishly, always expecting a personal share as a "cut." This jovial vice of a scramble for spoils flourishes in a wholly destructive atmosphere. In novel after novel the national legislature is painted as a corrupt body, its members willingly subscribing to this and that nefarious scheme.

Political figures, in and out of the legislature, are berated by the reform-motivated writers. There is the sleek, fraudulent John Andross created by Mrs. Davis, or Patrick Ballymolloy, the boss of the Massachusetts state legislature in *An American Politician,* or Brennan, the leader of the "third house" (the lobby) in *A Member of the Third House,* or his ward leaders Murnahan and Sheehan. Shoddy individuals all. Even the highly respected Congressman Harcourt of Myra Hamlin's *A Politician's Daughter* (1886) turns out to have a shady past.

Caleb Mason, the "hero" of David R. Locke's *The Dem-*

agogue, may well serve as a representative figure. From the first Caleb is seen as a young man on the make. He enters politics simply in order to make a good living. Capitalizing on his humble origins, then solidifying his position by a politically advantageous marriage, he moves rapidly ahead. In the state legislature he skillfully acquires an undeserved reputation for being incorruptible and uses his gift for oratory to gain prominence. He jumps on the antislavery bandwagon early, not from principle but because it is the "coming thing." He feigns a personal interest in his constituents, obtains control of the local newspapers, pulls wires to keep himself before the eyes of the voters (by riding the hobbyhorse of pensions after the Civil War and thus gathering the veterans behind him). In short, he does all the "right" things. By virtue of building up an elaborate political machine devoted to his interests, Caleb is able to move on to Washington as a representative. He almost goes on to even greater triumphs, a diplomatic post, but just at this point his past catches up with him, his shady deals become known, his selfishness and insincerity are exposed, his career is checked and he commits suicide.

Just as political personnel are singled out for attack, so, too, is the political machinery behind them. Many novelists point out that the system of nominating and electing candidates has drawbacks, mostly notably in that it fails to give proper expression of the popular will. Nominating conventions are operated by the few, the town and country bosses, or a tight little legislative caucus. These elect the presiding officers at such affairs and designate the key committees. And here, as elsewhere, party politics holds sway to too great a degree. The party lines are so strictly drawn that any candidate is considered "right" or any issue proper provided that he or it will pull the votes and thus entrench the party.

In the election process itself many evils crop up. The ballot box is stuffed; infant fatalities, in an "election-day resurrection," grow into voters; birth certificates get forged; "floaters" come to town for the occasion; brewery wagons are loaded with thugs who are trotted to the various voting booths to function as "repeaters"; poll watchers have laudanum put in their coffee. The machine runs smoothly but the methods are decidedly dirty.

Once the candidates are elected, the abuses do not necessarily disappear. Congressmen often do not function adequately in their legislatures, being too involved in mending political fences there and at home. Legislative bodies are often maneuvered by small groups of individuals. "Cannonism," the presence of an all-powerful Speaker of the House, may be in evidence, the Speaker appointing committees, referring bills, recognizing only those individuals whom he chooses to see, setting limits on debate, and so on.

The person who sets much of the political machinery in motion, the boss, provokes most of the ire of the writers. It is in this post–Civil War period that the popular brand of political fiction known as the "boss novel" makes its appearance. Books such as John Hume's *Five Hundred Majority* (1872), Rufus Shapley's *Solid For Mulhooly* (1881), J. M. Chapple's *Boss Bart, Politician* (1896) and Paul Leicester Ford's *The Honorable Peter Stirling* (1894) exemplify the trend. Except for Ford's account, these novels pillory the boss type. Since he is usually of nonnative stock (chiefly

Irish, though later, Italian or German), he is disqualified, in the eyes of many "gentlemanly" political novelists, from the outset. They also object to his authoritarian tactics, his tight control of the intricate party machine, and they consider him cruel and selfish, bestowing patronage only on the basis of service rendered—there is no benevolent largess—and not considering the welfare of the people at all.

In Hume's *Five Hundred Majority* the target is Tammany Hall, as directed from behind the scenes by Barton Seacrist. Although Seacrist is beset by problems such as the presence of a hostile press, uncertain support from the city's criminal element, a rival faction, the Mohicans, and even a newly created reform party, he wields immense power and rules successfully for some time. Although various opposition groups combine to defeat him at the end of the novel, most readers would anticipate Seacrist's speedy return to power. It had become almost axiomatic for the "Goo-goos"—as proponents of good government were then derisively labelled —to "turn the rascals out," only to have the rascals come romping back in the next election. An unhappy outlook, since the boss and his machine are "the plague of a free people."

Even more damning is Shapley's sketch of politician Mike Mulhooly and of the boss, Blossom Brick, who uses him. Brick heads a tightly organized "ring" which controls municipal politics, and he has considerable influence in the state as well. The "ring" selects the candidates for office, chooses the delegates to the convention which will "elect" the candidates, secures the chairman of the convention, runs the campaign (free drinks and many promises), and manipu-

34

lates the key figures such as newspapermen, lawyers, and judges. And the people? Brick has a precept for them: "Only make them think they rule and they are happy."

A quite different tack is taken by Paul Ford in *The Honorable Peter Stirling*. Supposedly modeling his protagonist on Grover Cleveland, Ford presents a "good" boss and, wonder of wonders, a man of good family, too. Peter Stirling, a "practical idealist," labors both astutely and unselfishly in the political arena, fighting for principles but knowing human frailties and of the need for occasional compromise. In sharp contrast to the Bricks and the Seacrists, he is primarily concerned about the welfare of the people whom he "bosses," and his machine runs for their benefit. Ford champions, then, a boss system of benevolent paternalism, more suited to improve politics, he feels, than the wild endeavors of visionary reformers. Although the novel makes some sensible points, its thesis is weakened by being developed through the incredibly stuffy and unbelievable Peter Stirling. The book carries a little more conviction than the tract-like *Five Hundred Majority* or the ponderously ironic *Solid For Mulhooly*, to be sure, and does serve the purpose of adjusting the balance on the subject of "bossism." The subject will be more thoroughly—and on the whole more perceptively—canvassed in the muckraking days ahead.

At the root of the evil in the American political system, as the writers of the postwar era see it, is the "grab for gold." This is demonstrated again and again: the greediness of the corporations (the railroad barons, as exhibited in T. S. Denison's *An Iron Crown* (1885), purchasing franchises from bribable legislatures, buying up the courts in order to obtain

35

tax exemptions, charging excess freight rates, and thus afflicting the "people"); the venality of Congress (franking clothes home free, as in *The Gilded Age*, or indulging in speculation under the guise of "internal improvement bills"); the paid press, which does not give a fair picture of the issues, and so on and on and on. Everyone seems to be affected, the intelligent, like Laura Hawkins and Henry Brierly in *The Gilded Age*, and the upright as well as intelligent, like Mr. Bolton in the same novel. In Henry Keenan's *The Moneymakers* (1885), almost everybody is scrambling after the loot, the railway magnate, the reporter, the customhouse collector, the senator, judges, architects—only "our hero," the good editor, holds out.

The political novelists sense, then, a widespread distortion of values in late nineteenth century America and are inclined, in the last analysis, to blame the people themselves for the political depravity of the time. Not "unconscious of wrong-doing," the public simply does not possess high standards; it condones underhanded practices, allows special privileges to be put before principles, and adheres blindly to the party line.

The reforms that the novelists suggest—after having delivered their philippics—prove mildly socialistic, or just mild. Mrs. Burnett counsels civil service reform, as does Crawford. Garland plumps for the Populists, urging a revolt, led by the farmer, against land monopoly (in *A Spoil of Office*). Twain and Warner and Keenan wish to lessen the mammon-worship. Myra Hamlin and David R. Locke want to lure good men rather than demagogues into the political arena.[7]

[7] The implications of Wilfred A. Ferrell's study of the political novels

The later novels of the period, as William Dickens has demonstrated,[8] reflect some dissatisfaction with *piece-meal* reform. Though individual problems are not ignored (e.g., women's suffrage in *The Women's Conquest of New York*, the power of the lobby in *A Member of the Third House*, machine control in *Boss Bart, Politician*), the trend is toward more sweeping proposals, such as the co-operative or socialistic states envisioned in Bellamy's *Looking Backward* and Donnelly's *Caesar's Column*. In every instance generalities rather than specifics rule, with the most universal cry urging the masses to assume civic responsibilities.

Although their efforts do not seem to have been directly influential, authors did contribute to the general groundswell of reform, out of which came, in the latter years of the nineteenth century, remedies such as the Australian ballot, as the designation of state officers to see that election laws were enforced, as antilobby laws, as municipal voters leagues, and fusion tickets. Thus, the way was paved for the even more active period of reform in the opening decade of the twentieth century.

The majority of the political novels published in the 1870–1900 span possess, one must unhesitatingly declare, more merit as propaganda than as art. Their chief, nay, al-

of this period are, however, that the demagogues continue to outnumber the "good guys." The politicians appearing in the sixty-one novels included in his study fit seven stereotypes: the rising young man, the rising young man who falls, aristocrat-politician, capitalist-politician, satirically ridiculous politician, corrupt professional politican, and leader of the people—two "good's" to five "bad's." See Wilfred A. Ferrell, "Portrait of the Politician in the American Novel: 1870–1910," unpublished Ph.D. dissertation, University of Texas, (n.d.).

8 Dickens, *op. cit.*, 21.

most their only, aesthetic virtue consists in their apt rendering of setting, of political "local color." Mrs. Burnett, in *Through One Administration*, graphically presents the Washington locale, concentrating on the social side, the receptions and balls, where so much of the politicking goes on. David R. Locke, in *A Paper City* (1879), stresses the rural political environment but summons up an equally clear picture, deftly painting the local rallies and county conventions which were such a source of entertainment for the village folk. Similarly, Myra Hamlin describes the county campaign and its chief weapon, the stump speech—three parts flattery of the locals and two parts orthodox views on silver, the tariff, and the civil service—which the "natives" lap up, as they do the election celebrations—torch-waving and apple-munching —depicted by Hamlin Garland.

While such on-the-scene authenticity pleases the reader, it does not enable him to forget the technical shortcomings of the novels. Their theses, however worthwhile, are explored in shallow fashion and marked by philosophical paucity. Their plotting proceeds along conventional lines, and the main political action often must vie for favor with an interfering sentimental romance. Narrative proportion is sometimes lacking (*q.v.*, the wrenched climax of *Five Hundred Majority*), and characterizations incline toward the superficial, with a pronounced hero-villain stereotyped division. Finally, the style of writing alternates between the journalistic and the stilted,[9] and the tone, in its obvious didacti-

[9] Jean Johnson offers an amusing parody: "He gazed upon her deep-red lips, sensitive and quivering in their dainty curving, while he talked of a minimum freight bill and the government ownership of railroads." See Johnson, *op. cit.*, 245.

cism,[10] sounds shrill. Gawky the novels are—and only partially redeemed by their clearly defined settings and by their vigorous exposé quality.

[10] F. Marion Crawford is an example, "obviously somewhat out of his element," says Mrs. Johnson, ". . . skirt[ing] the edges of the muddy political pool, trying with general moral exhortations to purify the waters without having to plunge in himself." See Johnson, *op. cit.*, 181.

☆

CHAPTER IV

Expertise: *Twain, De Forest, and Adams*

ACCORDING to general agreement, the most technically
proficient as well as the most interesting of the post-
Civil War political novels are Mark Twain and Charles Dudley Warner's *The Gilded Age* (1873), John De Forest's
Honest John Vane (1875) and *Playing the Mischief* (1875),
and Henry Adams' *Democracy* (1880). Although others appeal—*The Honorable Peter Stirling* in its sympathetic discussion of bossism, Howells' *A Hazard of New Fortunes* with
its unusual gamut of political views,[1] and the Populist novels
of Hamlin Garland because of their solid Middle Western
atmosphere—the fiction of Twain and Warner, De Forest,
and Adams has still higher claims, for it most closely approxi-
mates the needful blend of significance and art.

The earliest of the novels, *The Gilded Age*, resembles
most of its contemporaries in its decidedly sour analysis of
current political conditions. A pessimist rather than a hopeful reformer, Twain (to whom the political chapters of the
novel are universally attributed) expressed his disillusion-
ment with the corruption evident in the Washington political scene. One of the principal story strands deals with the

[1] Dryfoos the capitalist, his son Conrad the idealistic reformer, Colonel
Woodburn the agrarian, Lindau the socialist, and Basil March the uncom-
mitted moderate with a social conscience. *A Hazard of New Fortunes* is
most precisely described as an economic-political novel.

activities of such individuals as the hypocritical Senator Abner Dilworthy, Representatives Buckstone and Trollop, and lobbyist Laura Hawkins. These figures are involved in an attempt to maneuver through Congress the Knobs Industrial University Bill, one designed ostensibly to educate the Negroes but really to provide substantial sums of money for the Hawkins family and those assisting them. By some judicious bribing of the members of the appropriations committee, and by a little blackmailing, too, the bill's sponsors hope to secure its passage. Indeed, they almost do, despite newspaper denunciation and the outcry of a few honest individuals over the "swindle." But Laura Hawkins' involvement in a murder trial and Senator Dilworthy's exposure in an attempt to bribe his way to re-election put the quietus on their efforts. Not, however, before Twain has given ample evidence that public thievery is rampant in Washington, that for the failure of the Knobs University Bill, many another graft-laden appropriation manages to pass.

Twain severely indicts the moral climate in the national capital, a city inhabited by crooked congressmen, influence-peddlers and sinecure-seekers, a "fountain of patronage, preferment, jobs and opportunities." Everyone wants to get rich quick, usually by indulging in land speculation and by using "political influence." Congress receives the author's heaviest blows, almost every member having his price (despite its being masked under the guise of the "public interest"), and permitting himself abuse of the franking privilege and of his traveling expenses, as well as being guilty of the more serious offense of misappropriating public funds. When congressmen occasionally do investigate themselves, Twain cynically remarks, the performance proves merely "show"; no one is ever found guilty. Even Senator Dilworthy is white-washed.

Although impressive in its caustic and knowledgeable political sequences, *The Gilded Age* cannot be called an un-qualified artistic triumph. It displays, in fact, a decided un-evenness. This unevenness—probably attributable to the book's joint authorship—reveals itself most glaringly in the rickety structural pattern. The book's main plot (presum-ably Twain's contribution), the story of the Hawkins family and the disposition of their Tennessee land, occupies the cen-ter of the stage and involves the most interesting characters, Laura and Washington Hawkins, Senator Dilworthy and Colonel Sellers. The book's subplot (presumably Warner's contribution) outlines the love story of Ruth Bolton and Philip Sterling and introduces the less arresting personages.

As the book proceeds, plot and subplot are picked up and dropped, picked up and dropped, in what inevitably becomes an irritating fashion. Just as we find ourselves engrossed in the mystery of Laura's parentage, we must turn to Philip Ster-ling and his unrelated career. Just as the scene focuses on Washington and the promise of political exposure is held out, there is a backtracking to Ruth Bolton and her circle. Plot lines do cross occasionally, yet one always feels that he is reading two separate stories. The book as a whole rambles along, with a disproportionately long (and melodramatic) murder trial toward the end, and a sense of sprawl through-out; those two three-hundred-page volumes must be filled out. Perhaps one would not mind were the subplot of more interest; one cannot, however, follow its sentimental course (heroic rescues, sudden wealth, timely reunions) with breathless attention.

The book suffers also from occasional overwriting ("And a few critical years can decide whether her life is to be full of sweetness and light, whether she is to be the vestal of a holy temple, or whether she will be the fallen priestess of a desecrated shrine") and from auctorial intrusions ("It is impossible for the historian, with even the best intentions, to control events or compel the persons of his narrative to act wisely or to be successful"). The pep-talk passages and the stock characterization in the minor roles do not win the reader's approval either.

On the other hand, the political portions of *The Gilded Age*, the legislative sessions, for example, are effectively dramatized and presented in lively fashion. The Washington atmosphere "thick with speculation," the passage of appropriation bills, the adroitness of Senator Dilworthy's campaigning—descriptions of these carry conviction. One recognizes the Twain touch in the amusing satire on the gigantic schemes of Beriah Sellers, on the "adaptability" of Washington Hawkins, on lobbying in the national capital (mere merit, fitness and capability are useless baggage to you without "influence"), on the social pretensions of the wives of political figures. Obvious and extreme as the satire is ("it is telegraphed all over the country if a Congressman votes honestly"),[2] it achieves its purpose of arousing attention. Many of Twain's contemporaries must have thought twice as they

2 The authors, in a footnote attached to the scene depicting the visit of the Hon. Mrs. Patrique Oreillé (formerly O'Riley) to Laura Hawkins, declare that, "as impossible and exasperating as this conversation may sound . . . it is scarcely an exaggeration of one which one of us actually listened to."

read his scornful commentary on "representational government":

> In our cities the ward meetings elect delegates to the
> nominating conventions and instruct them whom to
> nominate. The publicans and their retainers rule the ward
> meetings (for everybody else hates the worry of politics
> and stays at home); the delegates from the ward meetings
> organize as a nominating convention and make up a list
> of candidates—one convention offering a democratic and
> another a republican list of—incorruptibles; and then the
> great meek public come forward at the proper time and
> make unhampered choice.

The leading characters are also an asset to the novel, the
sanctimonious Senator Dilworthy, the unscrupulous but fascinating Laura Hawkins, and the wonderfully bumbling but
goodhearted Colonel Sellers being memorably rendered,
and thus adding to the book's enjoyment as well as to its
worth. Senator Dilworthy seems at first glance a caricature,
the oily, hypocritical legislator, but in his loyalty to the
Hawkins family at the time of the murder trial he shows a
more positive side. Twain is bent on attacking the grafting
politician (Senator Samuel S. "Old Subsidy" Pomeroy is
supposedly Dilworthy's original), one who is venal and manipulating, yet his portrait is not limned entirely in black.

The same is true of the sketch of Laura Hawkins, for
whose villainy the author finds excuse in her uncertain parentage and unfortunate marriage. Laura as a lobbyist intrigues ruthlessly and just skirts the bounds of social re-
spectability, yet her self-realization—". . . a desperate game

44

I am playing in these days—a wearing, sordid, heartless game. If I lose, I lose everything—even myself. And if I win the game, will it be worth its cost after all?"—commends itself to us and makes her a poignant *and* human figure.[3] Colonel Sellers, somewhat poignant, too, in his Micawber-like qualities, wins the affection of most readers. Possessed of a tongue that is a "magician's wand," turning dried apples into figs, water into wine, turnips into a sumptuous dinner, he charms his way along. Bitten by the avarice of the time, not very discerning in his judgments, indeed, an ineffectual figure, yet he pleases by virtue of his good nature and his buoyancy.

The vigorous style and humorously ironic tone of what one again assumes to be the Twain segments (poor Warner!) of *The Gilded Age* are also praiseworthy. Colorful localisms, tart phrases (that "immaculate body" Congress), character-revealing dialogue, and pungent descriptions (such as that accorded Senator "Brother" Balaam) distinguish the style, and funny situations are sprinkled throughout the story: Colonel Sellers falling asleep in the Senate or elaborating upon one of his majestically proportioned schemes, Washington Hawkins endeavoring to square himself for a bow but only managing to put his foot through the train of Mrs. Senator Poplin, Laura Hawkins sweet-talking her way around Representative Trollop. The inimitable Twain flavor permeates the book and compensates, in large measure, for its mechanical weaknesses.

The only rather recently resurrected novelist John W. De Forest, in his political novels, covers similar ground as

[3] The authors themselves remark, "We are sorry we cannot make her a faultless heroine; but we cannot, for the reason that she was human."

Twain and Warner and, on the whole, more penetratingly. *Honest John Vane* and *Playing the Mischief* both deal with the corruption of the Grant era, the former presenting the unfortunate career of misguided Congressman John Vane, and the latter a study of the machinations of the lobbyist Josie Murray.

In the former fiction, the successful business man John Vane is persuaded to become a candidate for Congress to replace a representative from his district who has been caught taking a bribe. Vane, known as "Honest John" because he *once* turned down a shady proposal, seems a likely replacement. He secures the office as a compromise candidate, defeating the dishonest incumbent, and also a Mr. Saltonstall, who is too gentlemanly and too honorable to campaign successfully for the nomination. Active in advancing Vane's cause is Darius Dorman, a slimy lobbyist, who will subsequently entangle his steps.

Once in Congress Vane finds himself not too well equipped—or, rather, the reader finds him so. He has no knowledge of foreign affairs and very little of the internal workings of the government. In emphasizing his "darkmindedness with regard to American politics," the author editorializes about the need for the "gentleman," the man of good birth and breeding but mostly of good education, in the political field. De Forest objects to the too common American assumption that a man must be "self-made" in order to be worthy of the admiration or the vote of his fellow men.

More troublesome than his lack of knowledge to John Vane is the financial pressure exerted in Washington. Having found it difficult to live on his salary, especially since his wife wants to keep up with the early-day Mestas and Cafritzes, he begins to look for ways and means to supplement his income. Upon discovering that most senators and representatives get along comfortably by padding their pockets at any and every opportunity, he is disturbed and at first unyielding ("I won't go into your lobbying"). But economic pressures become too strong and consequently he heeds a proposal by Darius Dorman to take stock in the Subfluvial Tunnel Road (an underground road from the Great Lakes to the Gulf—why, nobody knows). An "inner" corporation masks the participation of Vane and other congressmen. Anyway, says Dorman at one point, if the graft is uncovered, Congress will go so far as to appoint an investigation committee, then succeed in hushing the matter up. From that stage on, Vane participates in numerous "deals"—as a shrewd businessman picking only the most profitable and safe—thus subverted by the capitalists working through their lobbyists.

The sobriquet "Honest John" has indeed acquired a hollow sound. Although partly victimized by his surroundings, Vane, so De Forest has implied from the first, must chiefly blame himself. He possesses a really "coarse soul" (Dorman spots him early as a chameleon), and in the unmoral atmosphere of Washington he has not a chance of keeping on the right road.

The seat of the national government is most grimly depicted. Lobbyists are everywhere at work, a "mammonite crew," some greasy thieves, some decayed statesmen, some dashing sports. The fraudulent claims which they advance mount through the sessions of Congress, reaching astronomical proportions. At the end of each session comes a flurry of legislation, each member bent on pushing his own pet project through and coining money from profitable arrangements. Honest bills, such as one opposing the franking privilege, are smothered in committee.

Eventually the public is aroused and demands an investigation of the Subfluvial fraud.[4] A few politicians are thus exposed, but John Vane manages to dodge and so to preserve his reputation. The "great, soft-hearted American public" is taken in by the "committee room whitewash." At the end of the book Vane is still riding high, and so are most of his equally soulless confreres. De Forest concludes:

> Nothing in the future is more certain than that, if this huge 'special legislation' machine for bribery is not broken up, our Congress will surely and quickly become, what some sad souls claim that it already is, a den of thieves.

Honest John Vane, though clearly built on a "cause,"

---

[4] This is De Forest's fictional version, says Joseph Rubin, of the *Crédit Mobilier* scandal. See John De Forest, *Honest John Vane* (State College, Pennsylvania, Bald Eagle Press, Monument Edition, 1960). (With an introduction by Joseph Jay Rubin).

Rubin's introduction, in addition to offering interesting comments on *Honest John Vane,* touches upon the history of the political novel genre. Citing *Modern Chivalry* and *Trumps* as among the few American guides prior to 1870, Rubin also speaks of possible English influences upon De Forest, notably Disraeli and Trollope. De Forest indeed refers to the latter's Parliamentary novels in *Playing the Mischief.* Rubin goes on to indicate the number of De Forest's contemporaries who became absorbed in the subject of politics, Twain, Adams, Tourgee, Garland, etc., all "attempting to master a fictional form and subject described by an English practitioner, Mrs. Humphry Ward, as most difficult of all but also the most tempting to the mature artist."

escapes the ponderous didacticism of the novel of purpose because the author, through his sketch of Congressman Vane, dramatizes his attack on the "juggernaut of swindling." Henry James's charge that the work should "pass as a tract for popular distribution"[5] must be challenged, for De Forest's use of a Congressional career to develop his antilobby thesis provides a subtlety of approach which a tract would lack.

Most instrumental in giving the book some distinction is the convincing presentation of the protagonist and his political role. John Vane initially attracts the reader as a capable manufacturer and as a good-looking and kindhearted man. At the same time De Forest carefully qualifies this favorable description, pointing out that Vane "ran a little too much to blubber for comfort" and had a face "slightly vacuous in its expression." As he enters the Congressional halls, he is seen as "an uninstructed soul" but "at all events an honest one." Like most humans, then, a mixture of strengths and weaknesses. He falls rather quickly "into the loose horde of Congressional foragers," to be sure, but even after becoming a deceitful spoilsman, he has moments of good sense and humility and moments when his conscience is revitalized.

De Forest carefully explains the inevitability of his downfall. John Vane never prized virtue for its own sake but because the name of it had brought him honor. His far-famed honesty really stood on the basis of egoism and vanity. Lacking the proper breeding and education which might have made him "a permanently worthy soul," he possessed instead

---

[5] Henry James, "*Honest John Vane*," printed in *Literary Reviews and Essays* (New York, Grove Press, 1957), 241. The review originally appeared in the *Nation*, Vol. 19 (December 31, 1874), 441–42.

"only the little, combustible block-house of vanity." Since this was hardly an adequate substitute for "moral sympathy," John Vane succumbed to the Washington pressure. The reader accepts his fall, but not without a measure of regret.

The novel's other principals, Vane's wife Olympia and lobbyist Dorman, are also sharply, if much less sympathetically, drawn. Olympia, a "true" characterization, as William Dean Howells said in his review of the novel,[6] appears as a handsome but vulgar individual, singularly devoted to things material ("she had a curious felicity at spending money, and did it literally without thinking"), and devoid of conscience. She proves a "greater trial and stumbling block than the lobby" to her husband, forcing him to join her in living well beyond their means.

The politician Dorman perhaps borders on caricature as De Forest tries rather too hard to liken him to the devil. First described as grimy and besmirched, with gripping claws for hands and an opaque finish of tint, he is then called a singed monkey, a bleached goblin, blurred, blotched, smoke-dried, with lurid, smoky eyes. He is finally seen as clasping blackened claws across his coatskirts, "perhaps to keep his long tail from wagging too conspicuously inside his trousers." When De Forest adds, "supposing he possessed such an unearthly embellishment," he obviously intends to joke

---

[6] The review, which appeared in the *Atlantic Monthly*, in February, 1875, is referred to in Joseph Rubin's introduction to *Honest John Vane*, *op. cit.*, 54. Howells, declaring that De Forest shows "the skill and force of a master," that "there has never been so good a political satire as this," differs immensely from James, whose review, in addition to labeling the work a tract, speaks of its turbid phrasing, heavily laid-on colors, and lack of delicacy (See footnote 5).

about Dorman in his Mephistophelean role, though not to relieve him of it. The lobbyist, if overly "satanic," is forceful in his shrewd malignity.

Honest John Vane recommends itself not only in its perceptive delineation of character but in other ways as well. It is a compact novel, devoid of subplots and irrelevant episodes, and for the most part lacking intrusions of the "let us not be severe upon the young lady because of her prudence" order. It is also well written. De Forest displays a gift for the neat phrase ("the widow of a wholesale New York grocer who had come out at the little end of the horn of plenty") and for vivid description (she "reminded one of those statues which travelers have seen in Italian court-yards. Once rounded, clean-cut and sparkling, but being of too soft a marble and beaten upon by winds and rain, they have lost distinctness of lineament and brightness of color").

He coins words effectively ("gallanted," "spiritual mobocracy"), or uses them in an unusual manner ("she had got a Congressman; but that almost continental fact did not satisfy her"). Fresh figures of speech appear (Vane avoided "pundits in constitutional law and Congressional precedent, whose deluges of political lore overflowed him like a river, and stranded him promptly on lone islands of silence"; "he still remained below the highest tidewater mark of vice [yet] got no foothold on the dry land of the loftier moral motives"), and interesting image patterns also; particularly striking are those of a military cast ("the guerillas of the lobby," "raids of special legislation"). The running series of allusions in the book to *Pilgrim's Progress*—Delectable Mountains, Christian, Faithful, Greatheart, Hopeful—re-

51

flect, one feels, the author's satiric inversion of the Bunyan allegory, a device to accentuate John Vane's reversal.

Throughout the novel De Forest acts as an angry observer of the current political scene. Scornful irony runs through his editorial statements (John Vane was too ignorant to be a teacher or professor, "but it was presumed that he would answer well enough as a law-giver for a complicated Republic containing forty millions of people"), he is hostile to most of his characters (there is more than greed of lucre in Darius Dorman's murky countenance; there is a longing to buy up honesty, character, self-respect, to purchase a soul), his imagery is dark (turkey buzzards, pigs, foul fireplaces).

Yet the tone of the work is lightened by the frequent bursts of humor, as in the picture of Olympia as "a veteran flirt, trained to tough coquetry in many a desperate skirmish," of John Vane telling "all that he knew about national politics, and some things which neither he nor any other man ever knew," or of his "genial" smile simpering "from desk to desk, like Hector's shield blazing along the ranks of Trojan warriors. . . . he proved himself the smiler of smilers." One recognizes the severe criticism of Congress implied in Dorman's advice to Vane—do not go into war memories and nigger worship, sentimental dodges which are played out. Go into finance, the only way to cut a figure in politics and to make politics worth your while—but one chuckles at the advice at the same time.

Playing the Mischief echoes the political sentiments of *Honest John Vane*, though De Forest's target shifts from the *Crédit Mobilier* affair to the claims lobby.[7] The author rues

[7] A seed for both novels is to be found in a short story, "The Inspired

the presence in Washington of the vast group of "claim-ants," Josie Murray, Mrs. Frances Warden, Jake Pike, Jack Hunt, and—a holdover from *Honest John Vane*[8]—Darius Dorman. He also objects to the Congressmen through whom they work: Representative Drummond, self-described as the agent of wirepullers and logrollers; General Bangs, noted chairman of the Committee on Spoliation; the bland General Hornblower; and the Honorable G. W. Hollowbread, trimmer.

Most of the people "inside Washington" must be de-scribed as amoral, engaging in audacious swindles, ruthless office-seeking, and dubious "special legislation." The ex-ceptions, Congressman Bradford, Colonel Murray, Senator Ledyard, and Representative Payson, the kind of people who "put their moral pocket-handkerchiefs to their noses when they see a private claim," stand out in sharp relief. All is wrong with a world, De Forest savagely reflects, in which they are so vastly outnumbered. Again he scolds the public. "When the industrious and virtuous cease to care for poli-tics," the Vanes, the Drummonds, and the Pikes will auto-matically come to the fore, men who regard lobbying as the "main-spring of statesmanship."

Since it exhibits some technical weaknesses, *Playing the Mischief* does not seem as competent a production as *Honest*

Lobbyist," about the machinations of one Ananias Pullwool, a tale which De Forest contributed to the *Atlantic Monthly* in December, 1872.

[8] Congressman Vane and his wife also turn up in *Playing the Mischief*, both very unflatteringly depicted.

In thus carrying over his characters, De Forest may have had the simi-lar practice of Trollope in mind. Rubin suggests that Trollope's Parliamen-tary series, in this and other ways, is paralleled by De Forest in his own "American Congressional series." See *Honest John Vane, op. cit.*, 45.

John Vane and therefore does not plead quite so successfully for political reformation. The reader grows bored at the succession of interviews about Josie's claim and at the repeated auctorial commentary. The interviews are too similar in format, the commentary, too overt ("It is the misfortune of one who writes the history of a claimant, that he can not be fastidious as to his company, nor give much space to personages of high worth"). The disquisitions on tangential issues, currency reform, agrarianism, feminism, and Darwinism, prove bothersome, too; interesting though they sometimes are, they serve as interruptions and are too prolonged.

The reader discerns flaws in the handling of setting and character as well. The "sets" could be more clearly realized. At the President's reception, for example, one is aware only of the huge crush of people and does not "sense" the locale, the rooms, the receiving line, or the protocol. Some of the characters could be more clearly realized, too. Since they are sketched in only one dimension, people like the stuffy Edgar Bradford, the "judicial" Belle Warden, and her flighty mother do not achieve much actuality. Nor does the collection of stereotypes in the background: the foppish Clay Beauman, the self-important Hamilton Bray, noisy General Bangs, corrupt banker Allchin, seedy editor Shorthand, bloomer girl Nancy Appleyard, and Jessie "Miss Appropriation" Cohen.

It would not be fair to overlook the book's many commendable features, however. One must grant its unity, for one thing. Although too long, the novel retains its focus, constructed as it is around the biography of Josie Murray. The plot develops logically, and suspense is built and maintained "by a series of probable and relevant hurdles placed in the steeplechase after the claim."[9] As Josie takes the hurdles, the reader encounters excellent scenes, such as Josie's wet ride with Hollowbread in the lost hack, the latter's proposal of marriage, and Nancy Appleyard's abortive attack on Drummond.

The novel does have some well-drawn characters, too. Individuals like the pathetic elderly Lothario Hollowbread, the thoroughly masculine Sykes Drummond, Rector Murray and his wife Huldah, the uncouth Jake Pike, and stern old Colonel Murray have what Howells called "inexorable veracity,"[10] as does the protagonist Josephine Murray. Josie is an intriguing blend of virtues and vices. She possesses beauty and wit, some womanly "delicacy and sensitiveness of perception." On the other hand, she is a liar and a mischief-maker, a born coquette, and an individual devoid of "moral discipline." She follows a risky course as she fights for her claim, playing off one individual against another, even engaging herself to two men at the same time! De Forest querying at one stage whether she could help her perfidies and duplicities, hints that Josie may be compulsively evil, really mentally ill. Certainly she proves a "millstone in petticoats," and one anticipates an unhappy end for her, despite her winning her claim. Her good nature, charm, and intelligence will not save her, accompanied as they are by greed, deceit, and instability.

Like *Honest John Vane, Playing the Mischief* is en-

---

[9] John De Forest, *Playing the Mischief* (State College, Pennsylvania, Bald Eagle Press, Monument edition, 1961) (With an introduction by Joseph Jay Rubin), 31.

[10] Quoted in *ibid.*

tertainingly written, offering, in fact, even more comic relief than its predecessor. Josie's verbal play with her suitors, the quips ("nothing could be charged against him except incompetence"), and the satiric jabs—Josie, theoretically mourning for her late husband, holds "a love of a lace handkerchief to her pathetic face"—promote laughter, as do the incongruous situations such as Mr. Hollowbread's catching Josie as she jumps out of a window—he does not find "the collision a pure joy."

To the author may be attributed considerable stylistic verve. He handles dialogue skillfully, the ponderous phrasing of Hollowbread contrasting with the aggressive talk of Colonel Murray, the badinage of Josie with the grammatical liberties of Jacob Pike. The set descriptions with which he introduces his characters succinctly pin down the individual, e.g., that of Sykes Drummond:

> He was about thirty years old, broad-shouldered, and otherwise strongly built, with a virile, audacious, trooper-like face, and a devil-may-care pugnacious bearing. His forehead was large, and over the eyes singularly prominent; his nose was Roman, and his chin vigorously defined, and his jaws powerful. His complexion was dark, pallid, and yet healthy; his black coarse hair was long and abundant. There was a fascinating expression of mirthful recklessness about his flexible mouth, which was the finest feature of his countenance, and was really handsome. On the whole, and taking into special consideration his appearance of puissant virility, he would be called an extremely good-looking man—at least by those who like the Robert-the-Devil type.

56

Images (the military again—the plan of campaign for the Presidential reception, the "ambushes of special legislation") and figures of speech ("in a very short time she had towed her venerable beau alongside the young man, although Hollowbread did not at all want to cruise in that direction"; "the wind blew tomahawks"; Beauman gazed at Drummond "with an impassive countenance, much as a Horse Guards swell might gaze at a forward grocer") dot the novel's pages, and so do literary allusions—to Dickens, Reade, Twain, Artemus Ward. De Forest's choice of words seems felicitous, whether he is coining (Hollowbread oratory as "balanced and Blaired"), repeating ("General Hornblower would not discuss the claim; he bowed it away, and waved it away and smiled it away"), being colloquial ("clean cracked"), or switching a word's use around ("litany" manner).

Because De Forest writes so engagingly here and in *Honest John Vane*, because he provides so many good scenes in both novels, and because he promotes his "message" with a reasonable degree of obliqueness through convincing focal characters, his work may be said to demonstrate the political novel in a finished form, and in my opinion it deserves the recognition which is finally being bestowed upon it.

Perhaps the most absorbing study of the Washington of the postwar period is afforded by Henry Adams' *Democracy*. Suavely ironic, stylistically accomplished, and provocatively reflective, it satisfies the critical reader, even though it is not an altogether flawless performance. Standing on the sidelines and not too happy there (were there to be no more Adamses as President?), the author throws out a sizable number of sharp observations about the national political scene on display before him. Ominous gloom emanates from him as he reflects on the "degradation of democratic dogma."

Silas P. Ratcliffe, senator from Illinois—"the prairie giant of Peonia"—serves as the villain of the piece, being a symbol for Adams of contemporary America, of democracy-as-it-is-practiced-today-in-America. A skillful orator, leader of men and a commanding figure, Ratcliffe has acquired leadership in the Senate and manages to retain it when he moves on to the Cabinet, maneuvering everybody including the President ("Old Granny," who is suspiciously like Ulysses S. Grant, as Ratcliffe is suspiciously like James G. Blaine)[11] to further his ambitions.

Ratcliffe, in pursuit of the charming widow Madeleine Lee, whose present purpose in life, we are told, is to get to the heart of the great American mystery, democracy and government, unfolds his political philosophy for her. Indulging in sophistries and sometimes in out-and-out lies, he establishes a convincing case, fascinating Mrs. Lee by his strong will and unscrupulous energy. Ratcliffe blames the people for whatever corruption exists in government, declaring that one must purify society and thus purify government. Then he describes the status quo in politics as he sees it. He is opposed to civil service reform, an ineffective and idealistic pro-

[11] Critics have shown that the novel has aspects of a *roman à clef*, the President being a composite of Grant and Hayes; Ratcliffe mainly Blaine; Carrington, James Lowndes; and Baron Jacobi, a portrait of the Turkish diplomat Aristarchi Bey. See Robert F. Sayre, *The Examined Self: Benjamin Franklin, Henry Adams, Henry James*, 68–69.

It is interesting to note that many political novels may be read in such a manner. A "key" to *Playing the Mischief*, for example, has been provided by Joseph Rubin. See De Forest, *Playing the Mischief*, 14, 16, 17.

ceeding, and one with no chance for success "so long as the American citizen is what he is."

Contrarily, he defends his position as a dedicated party man (and thus not averse to party patronage), insisting that many actions can be allowed in order to preserve the party in power. The fact comes to light, for instance, that he had allowed a vote fraud in a state election, justifying this as a means of insuring victory for his party. A win for the opposition, according to his rationale, would have meant a broken-up Union.

Ratcliffe thus embraces the doctrine that any means may be employed as long as the end is sound. He does not see the possibility of evil consequences stemming from such a doctrine, nor does he ask himself how far he is serving the party and how far himself. He speaks of the party in one breath ("Great results can only be accomplished by great parties") but of himself in the next (the pleasure of politics lies in the possession of power). Late in the novel, when he applies pressure on the President to put his supporters into key positions, he does so with an eye to his subsequent presidential candidacy.

Where, Madeleine Lee begins to wonder, does the *public* good enter at all into this maze of *personal* intrigue? She is at length forced to modify her conviction that under the scummy surface lies a healthy ocean current of honest purpose when she discovers that Ratcliffe had also in the past accepted a huge bribe from the Inter-Oceanic Mail Steamship Company. Although he glibly rationalizes again (the money had been given to the national committee, and, besides, "in politics we cannot keep our hands clean"), Mrs. Lee now sees him for what he is, one who shows a complete atrophy of the moral senses, and she realizes that she could never fulfill her earlier intention of "reforming" him.

Madeleine Lee, in her investigation of "democracy," is thus disillusioned to find men like Ratcliffe, ruthless opportunists, in control. She is also disturbed by the way the lobbyists swarm about Washington, and by their methods as explained to her by Mrs. Baker, the use of direct or indirect bribes, in the form of suppers and cards and theaters and wives. What she finds, in short, is that democratic government is not really that at all. The wishes of the people are not necessarily considered, and a tight little oligarchy rules.

Adams' dissatisfaction is reflected in his causing Mrs. Lee to withdraw to Europe and in his placing the other characters who tend to represent his point of view, Gore and Carrington, out of the main stream. The iron grip of party control is so disastrous and the citizenry are so often corrupt that this intelligent patrician all but rejects the democratic process. He views with the greatest of scorn the barbarians from the Middle West, "nature's noblemen," leading the "dance of democracy," a "danse macabre" to him.

Although a very amusing and a very revealing novel, still, as Robert Sayre remarks, *Democracy* "is something short of a good novel,"[12] failing to achieve this status chiefly for one reason. It is a novel *about* things rather than an imaginative recreation of them. Lacking the improvisatory skill of a thoroughly creative artist, Adams—like other novelists of ideas before him—appeals more strongly on intellec-

12 Sayre, *op. cit.*, 68.

tual than on emotional grounds. His principal characters are, in the last analysis, incomplete. As spokesmen for or against their creator's point of view, they remain fleshless, ideas rather than people. The Southern lawyer Carrington "stands for" the moral values of an age when politics was the domain of the gentleman. Gore represents cynicism, Ratcliffe, the principle of expediency. Even the protagonist, Mrs. Lee, is not full-bodied and does not seem to exist in a living world. The reader feels her to be the author, thinly disguised (the change of sex notwithstanding!), essayizing on what is wrong in Washington.[13]

Democracy has many grounds for appeal, however. It is, for one thing, neatly put together, proceeding from episode to episode (the Schneidekoupon dinner, the expedition to Mount Vernon, Lord Skye's ball for the Grand Duke and Duchess of Saxe-Baden-Hombourg) in brisk fashion, as it outlines the progress of the affair between Mrs. Lee and Senator Ratcliffe. In good order it mounts to its climax, the moment when Mrs. Lee rejects the senator and departs from Washington. The scenes along the way receive picturesque treatment, too, Mrs. Lee's opulent drawing room (Corot paintings, Persian and Syrian rugs, Japanese bronzes and porcelain), the Senate chamber, the British embassy.

Inasmuch as it dissects the Washington environment in a witty and sophisticated way, the novel may be said to resemble a comedy of manners, the author gently satirizing person and place. He mocks such figures as the "rather vulgar"

---

[13] One is inclined to question Mrs. Lee's "position." If, to Adams, the questing intellectual, to the reader, alas, she is a dilettante (*q.v.*, "at present she meant to see what amusement there might be in politics").

Congressman French and the lightweight State Department personnel (these "youthful diplomatists" danced and chirruped cheerfully "on the hollow crust of society, but they were wholly useless when one suddenly fell through and found oneself struggling in the darkness and dangers beneath"), and jollies such members of the foreign colony as Lord Dunbeg, befuddled by that Adams version of the "American girl, you bet," Victoria Dare.

He does not even spare his two principals, Silas Ratcliffe and Madeleine Lee, revealing the former to be manipulating, amoral, equivocal (yet also competent, powerful, a "big" man), the latter to be domineering, vain, shallow (she begins to skip the dull parts in the Congressional Record, then skips the whole), "hoity-toity" (yet also beautiful, intelligent, and witty). The customary Washington "occasions," such as Congressional sessions, Presidential receptions and legation balls, are rather maliciously described as well. Adams takes special delight in indicating the tendency on the part of a republican government to ape a monarchy—the homespun-as-homespun President and his shrewish wife attempt to have a "court" and in various ways imitate English royalty.

Throughout the book Adams writes with urbanity and polish. He often relies on good conversation, the thrust and parry of characters such as Baron Jacobi, Carrington, Senator Gore, and Victoria Dare permitting easy, indeed often sparkling, comment on social and political matters. The phrases are nicely turned ("Ruskin and Taine had danced merrily through her mind, hand in hand with Darwin and Stuart Mill"; Victoria Dare was "engaged to a coronet and a peat-bog, with Lord Dunbeg attached"), the irony accentuated by understatement ("The secret was that Mrs. Lee had artistic tendencies, and unless they were checked in time, there was no knowing what might be the consequences. But as yet they had done no harm"), the figures of speech surprisingly earthy (the senator from Illinois rose to this gaudy fly like a huge, two-hundred-pound salmon; characteristic of all senators is a boundless and guileless thirst for flattery, engendered by daily draughts from political friends or dependents, then becoming a necessity like a dram).

Usually the author retains a light tone ("In her despair she had resorted to desperate measures. She had read philosophy in the original German"), even when he is reproving. Yet he can become scathing when speaking of things political: "appointments" as the "absorbing business of government," the coarseness of the Presidential palate, and at times his voice grows shrill indeed—Who bids highest, who hates with most venom, who intrigues with most skill, who has done the dirtiest, the meanest, the darkest, and the most, political work?

Adams, it is transparently clear, joins Twain and De Forest in reflecting a feeling that the American democratic experiment has been spoiled by the almost perpetually sordid political environment. They all look back nostalgically on the democracy of an earlier America when "gentlemen" were chosen to steer the government. Beyond this "exposure" of the infamous side of politics and this affirmation of the need for principled leaders, they, in their "studies," really do not go. Perceptive though Henry Adams is, for example, he fails to take into account the effect of economic factors—the industrialism of the East and the agrarianism of the West—on political practices, and his contemporaries show similar short-sightedness. All three, Adams, Twain, and De Forest, however, introduce some reasonably complex political figures into their fiction and at the same time tell their tales with dexterity, thus giving solidity and value to their version of the political novel.

CHAPTER V

The Heyday (1900–1920)

THE American political novel enjoyed its greatest vogue in the first decades of the twentieth century. Popular then, as earlier and later, because politics seems to touch society at almost every point and because all individuals are concerned, or should be, with political affairs, it was especially popular from 1900 to 1910 owing to the reform spirit of those years. The form, which has at times been avoided as being too "unlovely," echoed the muckraking temper and, like exposure journalism, eschewed the "syrup" (to be sure, the sentimental love story still crept in), which for a while audiences did not demand. It was a time of ferment and insurgency; a progressive spirit filled the air and brought on a national interest in reform. Speaking to this interest, many and many a novelist expressed his fears that legislators had forgotten they held a public trust and his belief that the lawmaking machinery needed overhauling.

The desire for political reform expressed itself along three general lines: an insistence that corrupt influences in national, state, and local governments be removed, a demand for modification of the machinery of government in order to guarantee rule by the many rather than by the few, and a call for an increase in governmental power to relieve social and economic distress. The people were becoming conscious that the growing power of the "bosses" had laid bare evils in our political democracy and that the growing power of the business corporations had laid bare evils in our economic democracy, and in both cases that a "public be damned" attitude prevailed.[1]

Protests were voiced principally by three different types of people: the young journalists such as Lincoln Steffens and David Graham Phillips; the political leader reformers like Missouri Attorney General Joseph Folk, Samuel "Golden Rule" Jones of Toledo, Cleveland Mayor Tom Johnson, Judge Ben Lindesey of Denver, and Theodore Roosevelt; and the political novelists like Winston Churchill, Elliott Flower, Brand Whitlock and the doubling-in-brass Phillips. All three types proved more photographic than interpretative, but certainly they—for the time being—cleared the air.[2]

Even a brief survey of the events of the pre-World War I era cannot fail to show numerous "progressive" spirits at work and their protests bearing fruit. The muckrakers, one might say, were overdue. The preceding period had been one of upheaval, with the farmer suffering misfortune and the laborer, too, in fact, all but the big captains of industry and the politicians in league with them. The latter two groups handled the "business government" of the country,[3]

---

[1] William K. Vanderbilt's famous phrase is echoed in one of the political novels of the time. See Charles K. Lush, *The Autocrats* (1901), 54.

[2] "Their achievement in highlighting corruption in politics and the darker phases of American society furnished a basis in conviction for the national effort to achieve government representative of the people and responsive to their social and economic needs." Arthur S. Link, *American Epoch*, 78.

[3] In the words of Lila and Arthur Weinberg, ". . . wealth flourished in its domination of politics, and political corruption was a daily love affair

the corporation wielding great power and the general public remaining inert. Many symptoms of unrest had manifested themselves in the 1880's and 1890's, and the way was thus paved for the appearance of reformers who would expose evils and corruption and attempt to promote righteousness and social justice.

That "damn cowboy,"[4] Theodore Roosevelt, must be regarded as a key figure in the 1900–10 "protest" decade, though he himself was no muckraker and indeed, in applying the term to the Steffens coterie, did not intend to be flattering (not being fully in agreement with their methods of exposure). Yet, with his gusto and moral enthusiasm and his concern for the lot of the unfortunate, he epitomizes the progressive temper and aim. Roosevelt's political career has reform associations, of course. He had been "kicked upstairs" into the Vice-Presidency from the governorship of New York by Senator Tom Platt, the New York state boss, because of his reforming tendencies and refusal to co-operate with the "machine." When McKinley's assassination elevated him to the Presidency, thus removing him from the obscure shelf where Platt thought him snugly placed, he was given a golden opportunity to set forth his reformist notions.

In his first message to Congress he laid down his plank: greater regulation of trusts, extension of the powers of the Interstate Commerce Commission, and an emphasis on a national conservation policy. A conservative Congress yielded

between big business and the big political boss." Arthur and Lila Weinberg, *The Muckrakers*, xiii.

    [4] Mark Hanna's epithet. See George E. Mowry, *The Era of Theodore Roosevelt, 1900–1912*, xi.

to *some* of his demands, permitting him to secure, for example, indictments of the beef trusts and others. Carrying on after his 1904 election, Roosevelt obtained the passage of the Hepburn Act, railway-rate regulation, and, with a large assist from Upton Sinclair—*The Jungle* was one political, or, as I prefer to call it, economic novel which clearly effected reform—the passage of the Pure Food and Drug Act.

Yet his actual achievement does not loom large (his administration brought fewer suits against monopolies than Taft's), for, though his sympathies lay with the middle and lower class "victims," he had no intention of destroying the power of the great industrialists and financiers. He also realized that he had to deal *with* the political bosses and deal *in* political favors. A reformer, yes, but a politician, too. Not even a reformer in the eyes of the uncompromising Lincoln Steffens. Roosevelt, he declared, "was not a reformer in the White House; he was a careerist on the people's side."[5]

Roosevelt seems to have set the ball rolling, however, and reforms continued under Presidents Taft and Wilson. In the former's administration business combines were prosecuted, the power of the Speaker of the House, autocratic Joe Cannon, was limited, and the question of excessive campaign expenditures was reviewed, if not solved. Wilson, in his first four years in office, secured the lowering of the tariff, trust regulation, an income tax amendment, and the ratification of the amendment providing for the direct election of senators.

Most important in encouraging the passage of such amendments, in rectifying other abuses, and in stimulating the movement for reform generally were the "muckrakers."

[5] Quoted in Stewart H. Holbrook, *Lost Men of American History*, 303.

From 1902 to 1911, they continually stirred up the social conscience of the people, succeeding, by means of the popular magazines in which their articles appeared, in reaching the majority of the citizens.[6] Lincoln Steffens, Ray S. Baker, Ida Tarbell, Thomas Lawson, Samuel Adams, and a host of others began to lay bare various national evils, corruption in government, the injustice of big business control ("frenzied finance," in Lawson's phrase), the unsavoriness of the patent medicine market, trickery in advertising and in the field of life insurance, and so on. Factual and accurate and on the whole dispassionate, the journalists showed conditions as they were, though offering few remedies.

Others provided the remedies, however. After Lincoln Steffens had pointed out the "shame of the cities"—their petty police graft, business and boss control—reforms in municipal governments were made. Galveston, for example, introduced a commission plan of government to replace the mayor and his council, and other cities turned to the city manager plan. This was the era, too, for reform mayors like Jones and Whitlock and Johnson, and for shaking the hold—temporarily, at least—of the bosses, Magee in Pittsburgh, Lomasney in Boston, Butler in St. Louis.

Steffens had also demonstrated the weaknesses of state government, where elaborate systems of bribery prevailed

[6] As many a historian has stated, the literature of exposure was not anything new. Many premuckraking novels as we have seen, were published in the late nineteenth century, and nonfiction "tracts for the times" as well. What *was* new was the existence of a group of writers and a concentration of magazines through which they might voice their opinions. These opinions reached a large public, one ready to hear the "press agents" for progressivism, and even to agitate for change, though never to agitate enough to suit the firebrand publicists.

and where governors were merely pasteboard men. As a consequence, changes were introduced in this area as well. Leaders like Robert LaFollette in Wisconsin, Charles Evans Hughes in New York, and Hiram Johnson in California engineered corrective action such as the initiative and referendum and right to recall officials and the curbing of excessive expenditure of money in elections.

Finally, Steffens had indicated flaws in the national government, particularly in the Senate, backing up David Graham Phillips, who had aimed at the same target more flamboyantly in a series of articles called "The Treason of the Senate." Assailing this rich man's club, Phillips cited such as Chauncey Depew, a member of seventy boards of directors, from which he received fifty thousand dollars a year in attendance fees, and Nelson Aldrich, the "right arm of the interests." Reforms here came more slowly, but eventually the Seventeenth Amendment offered some amelioration.

The muckrakers, it is true, presented a relatively narrow scope of experience and a somewhat shallow philosophy, yet they performed a valuable and necessary service in freely and caustically criticizing the men in power and in prodding the mass of Americans out of their lethargy. Their "publicity" gave new power to demands for railroad legislation, vice investigation, modification of election procedures, and elimination of many another existing evil.

It is chiefly by way of the muckrakers that we can trace the connection between this progressive movement toward reform and the political novel of the period. The muckrakers performed three services. By arousing interest in the operations of politicians and businessmen, they created an audience for the novel of politics and business. They revealed to novelists the dramatic value in the lives of great financiers and bosses. And they offered models for a realistic, factual technique. The road from exposé journalism to exposé fiction is short and straight.

In those aroused days of the opening years of the twentieth century, it became *the* fashion to write novels of reform. Edward Eggleston turned from *The Hoosier Schoolmaster* to report, in *The Mystery of Metropolisville* (1900), on the political maneuvering involved in the still popular Western game of land speculation. Mary E. W. Freeman put aside her local color stories to deal with the problem of labor unrest in *The Portion of Labor* (1901). Alfred Henry Lewis forsook his Wolfville stories of cowboy life to write *The Boss* (1902) and *The President* (1904). Ellen Glasgow jumped on the bandwagon with *The Voice of the People* (1900), and Edith Wharton, with *The Fruit of the Tree* (1907). Professional politician Brand Whitlock not so surprisingly joined the procession (*The 13th District,* 1902), and so, too, English professor Robert Herrick (*The Memoirs of an American Citizen,* 1905) and Booth Tarkington, beginning his career (*The Gentleman From Indiana,* 1899). Even Winston Churchill effected a change of direction, shifting from the historical romance to the "progressive novel." About this switch Vernon L. Parrington remarked: "There is something pathetic in the way the harmless bleating romantics were dragged at the chariot wheels of social problems."[7] But Parrington's phrase is more colorful than accurate. Churchill

[7] Vernon L. Parrington, *Main Currents in American Thought,* 3, p. 348.

had been heading toward the novel of realism and an accurate rendering of the current social scene for some time.

As one examines their "wares," he soon discovers that the early twentieth century political novelists single out for attack very much the same targets as those set up by their predecessors, and even offer parallel solutions. Their treatment seems more knowing, however, their view of politics and politicians more detailed and exact. Most of the "press agents for the Progressive Movement"[8] spoke with an easy authority.

In their talk of political life, these "angry young men"— and women—often focused on the "boss system." Since the power of the political boss had reached its zenith at the turn of the century, this attention is not surprising. The boss system theoretically operated on the local level, chiefly in the big cities, where "the man" controlled the police force, lawyers and courts, the public service corporations (by his power of granting franchises), and of course the somnolent electorate which gave him his power and which he held by perennial charities and carefully distributed patronage. Tammanyite Charles F. Murphy offered a living example to the novelists, the uneducated but sagacious leader, adaptable— and with the patience that outlasts every "reform." Tammany, despite having encountered various reversals, still flourished at this time, a tremendously scientifically organized machine, with the wheels constantly oiled by the distribution of jobs, the sale of favors, fraud at the polls, and its own naturalization techniques. There were lesser oligarchies

---

[8] Weinberg, *op. cit.*, xviii.

in cities other than New York, too, in Philadelphia and San Francisco, for example, where the usual practices of ballot-box stuffing, extortion of money from restaurants and saloons, levying of assessments on municipal employees, and selling franchises to wealthy corporations continued blithely. The "system" always bounced back after the exodus of the reform mayors.

The "boss" becomes a favorite character among the novelists, as Churchill's Jethro Bass and Job Braden, Whitlock's Jim Rankin, Phillips' Harvey Sayler, F. C. Williams' Jimmy Devlin, Ellen Glasgow's Major Rann, Alfred Lewis' Big John Kennedy, and the nameless leaders in Elliott Flower's *The Spoilsmen* (1903) and Mark Lee Luther's *The Henchman* (1902) testify. These undercover men control the political scene, from the Throne Room at the Pelican Hotel, or from a Third Avenue saloon, or from a nondescript business office, and it is they who make the candidates, conduct the campaigns, and steer the legislative bodies.

Although sometimes merely background figures in their particular novels, the bosses more often play leading roles. Francis Williams' *J. Devlin, Boss* (1901) focuses on the titular character, following his career as he forges ruthlessly ahead from humble beginnings to become the boss of New York City. At first one of a triumvirate, Jimmy Devlin subsequently ousts his "partners" and ends in sole control of a close-knit machine. Its members, the city council, the "Water Trust," and several state officials, are all prepared to do his bidding. Big John Kennedy in Alfred Lewis' *The Boss*, advances in similar fashion ending up in control of

73

the polls, the police and the people, running a huge graft system which benefits himself largely, and waiting out the occasional reform forays until a return to power is feasible.

Despite their lust for power, several of the bosses appear in a remarkably sympathetic light. Jimmy Devlin shows himself honest to individuals and kind to the masses. Rankin in Whitlock's *The 13th District* possesses redeeming traits, which win for him a larger share of the reader's approval than that garnered by the shabby Congressman "hero" Jerry Garwood. Although wary and cynical and not averse to buying up votes and shanghaiing nominating conventions, he is faithful to his bargains and loyal to his friends. The quiet and intelligent "boss" in *The Henchman* earns more respect than the book's rambunctious protagonist Ross Shelby, even after the latter "verges on statesmanship" and thus away from the machine. In like manner Tarkington's Boss Gorgett (*In the Arena*, 1905) merits more praise than the egoistic reformer Knowles. Paul Leicester Ford's prototype of the "good boss" in *The Honorable Peter Stirling* had, one concludes, left its mark.

Mrs. Jean Johnson ascribes the popularity of this "good boss" concept to the American tendency to idealize the ordinary man who "gets on," and to view him, after he has risen to power, as a lovable rogue or twentieth century Robin Hood.[9] Conveniently forgotten in the process is the fact that, while the boss distributes largesse to the bewildered immigrant and the tenement dweller, he retains a very substantial amount for himself.

Mrs. Johnson also makes the interesting assertion that,

[9] Johnson, *op. cit.*, chapter 4.

as the boss rose in public esteem (and in the esteem of the political novelists), the reformer fell. In Warren's *The Land of the Living* (1908), Colton's *Port Argent* (1904), Robertson's *The Opponents* (1902) and Luther's *The Henchman,* the reformer figures appear simply as men of words, not deeds, and in each of these books a woman turns to the red-blooded politician in preference to the "men of words." Brand Whitlock, politician as well as novelist, said: "I came to know both species pretty well, and, in the later connotations of the term, I prefer the politician. He, at least, is human."[10] As these comments suggest, the reformer was thought to lack sympathy for humanity, to deal in abstractions rather than in people. Moreover, his effect was so temporary; one character in Lewis' *The Boss* likens it to a drunkard signing the pledge but taking no notice of the pledge thereafter.

The most potent deterrent to permanent reform was not the detachment of the reformer type, however, but rather the hold exerted by the business interests over the government and the lure of monetary success in the minds of the people. As Charles Lush asserts in *The Autocrats,* it is money that makes the wheels spin around—just as in the preceding age. The boss, we discover, usually controls the political scene with the assistance of the corporation—the railroad, the oil company, the public utility. The "special interests" supply the money for campaigns, select tools as candidates,

[10] From Brand Whitlock's *Forty Years Of It,* quoted in Johnson, *op. cit.,* 277.

An exception to the pattern may be noted in Mary Dillon's *The Leader* (1906), whose hero, a magnetic and dynamic reformer and man of action, is distinctly human and is loved by the people. What is more, he gets the girl.

often even rule the courts. The Western Pacific Railroad in Francis Lynde's *The Grafters* (1904), for example, uses passes and bribes of other sorts to influence legislators. Big businessmen defended this corporation rule with various kinds of cant. They rationalized that it was a matter of protection; they must have a sympathetic legislature or else be shorn of power. Or they declared that their concern was for the interests of their stockholders. But basically it was another illustration of the survival of the fittest (as is very evident in such a book as Theodore Dreiser's *The Titan*),[11] with the strong captains of industry carefully smoothing out their paths by buying the legislators.

Since many legislators are thus paid agents, one need not expect an honest performance from the lawmaking assemblies to which they belong. An example of their functioning is seen in Winston Churchill's account of the "woodchuck session" in *Coniston* (1906). The Speaker of the House, Heth Sutton, does the bidding of the boss and/or corporation; various factions vote "down the line" (their votes already having been purchased); committees sit on bills which they wish to kill, introducing them only when there is a well-nigh empty house; the few honest representatives are relegated to the back row and, unversed in parliamentary procedure, are quite overwhelmed. Similarly, Humphrey Crewe, in Churchill's *Mr. Crewe's Career* (1908), is kept off important committees, where he might bring about

[11] Robert Herrick's *The Memoirs of an American Citizen* offers another example, in its Nietzschean superman Van Harrington, who competes and bribes without scruple, though remaining true to his own tough-minded code of personal responsibility and productive work.

some reforms, and witnesses the burial of any worthwhile measures which do threaten to appear before the legislature.

This picture of the New Hampshire state legislature has its counterpart in Washington. The Senate, a "millionaire's club of vested interests," is filled with malpractices, and the House of Representatives lags not far behind. Some Congressmen buy their way into office, in the first place, and sell their vote thereafter. Senator Hanway in Lewis' *The President* reveals the standard pattern. A man with the "countenance of a prelate and the conscience of a buccaneer," he grafts shamelessly to increase his own fortune at the expense of the public good, and he manipulates his fellow Congressmen to secure the appointment of a "tool" as the Speaker of the House and thus to further his presidential ambitions. A "statesman" to Senator Hanway is a "dead politician."

A reasonably thoughtful analysis of the Washington environment is provided in Gertrude Atherton's *Senator North* (1900). Socialite Betty Madison, running counter to the principle that women should not interest themselves in politics, especially society women (Congressmen are social upstarts), explores this world, much as Madeleine Lee had before her. Informed by her cousin Jack Emory, on the one hand, that not an honest man is to be found in politics, and informed by Senator Burleigh, on the other, that corruption is much less widespread than generally assumed, Betty decides for herself that the handful of senatorial *leaders* are admirable men, magnetic, intelligent, honest. Witness the New England senators who come back term after term because they have convictions and the courage to uphold them.

Although recognizing the presence of many weaklings in the Senate, and of corrupting elements (lobbyists and bosses and faulty electioneering methods) on the fringes, she feels that control of the Senate rests safely in the hands of the "paragons" (operating mostly in committee rooms). As long as this aristocracy of talent dominates, all will be well. Betty Madison's—and presumably Mrs. Atherton's—view really represents a throwback to the Fenimore Cooper position.

In other novels the picture of congressional Washington is more savagely drawn. There appear plausible but deceitful lobbyists, the "hearing lice" who filter in and out of the Capitol, making young and upright Congressmen a particular prey. There appear not so upright Congressmen, like Phillips' Joshua Craig (*Joshua Craig*, 1909), a selfish and shrewd individual, who arrives in high places by his clever catering to his constituents, and, once there, finds himself in shoddy company (the attorney-general is weak, the secretary of the treasury unprincipled, the President timid), where he is quite at home. The scramble for loot and the scramble for social precedence[12] disfigure the environs of Capitol Hill as well.

Some of the worst abuses crop up in the functioning of the political machinery, chiefly the nominating and electing of candidates procedure. Here the "bosses" take direct

---

[12] Money madness permeates books such as Lewis' *The President* and Phillips' *The Cost* (1904), and the social game is well described in Robert Grant's *Unleavened Bread* (1900). The latter's heroine, Selma Lyons, coming to Washington with her congressman husband, expects to be treated royally—even if equality is the essence of American doctrine—but finds that political and social prominence in Washington are by no means synonymous.

control, lining up votes, getting the delegations pledged, and running the nominating conventions. A weakness of the representative system of government becomes apparent in that the delegates to the convention more often represent the powers-that-be than they do the people. Candidates, chosen by the machine or the corporations, are endorsed automatically by the delegates, then secure their election by various kinds of "deals," bribing, boodling, coercing, indulging in malicious campaigning, by, for example, buying up the press, which will then malign the opposing candidate.

Supporting the candidate is the country's fundamental political organization, the party. In the United States the two-party system prevails, with splinter groups hardly counting. A bitter struggle is waged between the two in the pages of various political novels. When one group is in, it is *in*, distributing patronage and other favors (political "troughsmen" still abound), and the other group might as well move for the time being to Timbuktu. Strict party lines are drawn and rigid discipline maintained, with authority resting in the hands of a few, the boss, the lawyer representing the corporation, or sometimes the corporation head himself (as John Barclay in William Allen White's *A Certain Rich Man*, 1909). This "ruler" usually occupies a key position, e.g., as head of the state party committee—though he may use a "front" for this—through which he manages with perfect precision. Harvey Sayler in Phillips' *The Plum Tree* acquires so much power that he can even select the opposition candidate—choosing a weak one, naturally. Equally powerful is John Barclay in White's novel, directing the state legislature through his "agent" Lige Bemis, giving out railroad

79

passes strategically, keeping a card index on the politicians, with their strengths and weaknesses carefully catalogued. Barclay's conception of the party—it is to protect the men who support it, not necessarily the people as a whole—sums up the prevailing attitude.[13]

Now, where does John Q. Public fit into all this? Quite simply, he does not. John Barclay, as we have just seen, is concerned only with the strong few, and declares that the party is also. This is *not* a people's government, not a democracy, not a representative system (n.b., Churchill's Asa Gray, who wants, as the author puts it, to represent the Northeastern Railroad in the United States Senate). The so-called "People's Party" in Lynde's *The Grafters* is manipulated for the benefit of the "conscienceless demagogues" who run it, and in *The President* the electorate is constantly hoodwinked by senators and representatives, even by the President himself.

Most of the writers agree that the people must take the blame upon themselves, however. If more receptive than in the preceding era, the ordinary citizen—so claim the novelists —still does not take enough interest in his government, allowing bribery to go on, the corrupt officials to rule, not attempting to secure good men for office and then to elect them, minding the scandal more than the corruption. The passive and resigned voters in Tarkington's *The Gentleman From Indiana* exemplify the attitude of indifference.

---

[13] Barclay resembles Herrick's Van Harrington, another intellectual without moral restraint, using any means to the end, allowing a multitude of sins to creep in as he supposedly pursues the "larger good."

Winston Churchill utters a dissenting note at the end of *Mr. Crewe's Career,* when he suggests that the masses *have* awakened to the need for reform. His less optimistic contemporaries, however, refuse to find much civic awareness. The masses in *The Henchman* see politician Shelby as a colorful man of the people, not as a packer of caucuses, stealer of speeches, jobber of contracts, and groveler to the Boss; the "unco guid" people in *The Memoirs of an American Citizen* shun wicked Van Harrington but show no signs of revolting against the kind of thing he has done; the "better class" in Thomas Nelson Page's *John Marvell, Assistant* (1909) do not revolt against the robber barons, the political bosses, the shyster lawyers, and the lying press. Only the unworldly minister John Marvell and the Jewish socialist Wolffert register protests.

Relatively few remedies counterbalance the long list of political ills exposed by the novelists of the muckraking era. The authors, echoing a long-standing theory, declare that the electorate must put good men into office, gentlemen, not politicians, but they do not demonstrate much faith in this goal's being accomplished. Seeking the "expert," they discover even this breed to be tainted by the "grab for gold." The "plum tree" is shaken by vast numbers, and wealth and power substitute for "social morality."

The political novelists at least pointed the way toward the ideal, and they were shrewd enough to know that politics can not be set right in a hurry, if not shrewd enough to have all sorts of concrete suggestions (Upton Sinclair has one—socialism—and Thomas Nelson Page, that true-blue Southern gentleman of all people, flirts with the same idea). Perhaps that is as much as we have a right to expect.[14]

We have more right to expect from them a large measure of fictional talent, but, unfortunately, the measure is not forthcoming. Most of the political novels of the period, one must quite unequivocally state, possess little aesthetic merit.[15] Since many—those of David Graham Phillips, for one— result from a journalism-fiction combination, they illustrate the faults of the "reporter's novel," seeking to get by on an accumulation of detail, together with a little indignation and not much thought. They propagandize rather crudely, without a proper selectivity of material and without a dramatization of the presentation (the problem novel, as Pattee reminds us, "must carry other freight than its problem").[16] Most of the novels display an uncertain blend of new incidents (political scenes) with ancient formulas (boy-meets-girl, boy-loses-girl, boy-gets-girl), a mixture of realism and

[14] Wayne Burns reminds us, "As artist, the novelist cannot solve social and moral problems; his sole responsibility is to his humanness and his art." Wayne Burns, "The Novelist as Revolutionary," *Arizona Quarterly*, Vol. 7 (Spring, 1951), 27.

[15] The critical chorus joins in: ". . . one of the simplest literary genres that ever existed" (Henry F. May, *The End of American Innocence*, 23); "as literary craftsmen Brand Whitlock, Alfred Henry Lewis, David Graham Phillips, and Winston Churchill were perhaps not too far above the level of the popular historical romances . . ." (Mowry, *op. cit.*, 32); ". . . the works of every kind that sprang from the muckraking circle were superficial, among them the scores of political novels . . ." (Van Wyck Brooks, *The Confident Years, 1885–1915*, 386); "The muckraking novels are better social documents than literature. Their authors were too angry and too intent on reform by disclosure to pay much attention to the probabilities of plot and the intricacies of character. But their contribution to American life was not negligible" (Willard Thorp, *American Writing in the Twentieth Century*, 17).

[16] Fred L. Pattee, *The New American Literature, 1890–1930*, 151.

sentimentality which is not overly palatable. They disregard, as Willard Thorp rightly remarks, "probabilities of plot and the intricacies of character." Ellen Glasgow, for example, simplifies the upward struggle of Nick Burr, her hero in *The Voice of the People,* and thus detracts from the book's verisimilitude. Style, too, is perfunctory and "Sunday supplementish," and often the books seem overwritten, the fierce reforming spirit of the authors carrying them into emotional excesses and away from intellectual solidity.

Mark Lee Luther's *The Henchman* may serve as our whipping boy to prove this lack of artistry. The book adopts the standard biographical pattern, following the career of Ross Shelby as he mounts the political ladder to the governorship of New York. Although this is a perfectly satisfactory pattern from a structural point of view, still, the book has a "huddled" quality, for the protagonist acts, until the final pages, like a typical conscienceless politician, then is too suddenly converted. The author, one feels, should have devoted more time to authenticating this conversion. Granting that Shelby demonstrates a strong character and some appealing traits from the outset, yet he is pre-eminently the demagogue, and thus his taking the high road of statesmanship at the end fails to convince. We feel an imbalance in the structure and of course a flaw in the characterization.

Luther also masses the facts, describing Shelby's actions and his associates in excessive detail, rather than selecting key scenes to reveal character and dramatizing the conflict between moral and "political" codes. Admittedly, the background conveys a complete sense of actuality, the ratification of candidates meeting, the stumping tours, the activities of the state boss (deftly getting rid of a threat from kid-glove reformers by dumping one into the cabinet, making another a plenipotentiary, and sending a third on some commission to the other side of the world), but it could have been more lightly sketched in with the same effect of realism achieved.

The novel unfolds the omnipresent love story, this time with a double set of lovers complicating matters. Shelby fails to marry his true love, who falls to the lot of a colorless reformer type, instead he marries an ambitious and unscrupulous widow. Neither marriage is happy. Although this unusual unhappy-ending twist provides interest, one's sympathy is lessened because of the rather arbitrary balancing off of the quartet, *the pure* versus *the fleshly woman, the red-blooded* versus *the coldly intellectual man.* The combinations would be susceptible to some psychological exploration, but Luther does little with them.

He also makes little pretence at literary style. If now and then a good phrase can be found—"a man of tactless integrity," "practical politics is applied human nature"—such is the exception rather than the rule. More often the descriptions, whether of place or character, ooze embarrassingly: "It fell a ripe autumn day with the haze mantling the orchards like the purple of a plum, a day in whose magic atmosphere even common things wore an air of poetry. The very canal was transfigured."—"Some men the cassock effeminates; not so North, whose virile shape it emphasized, modeling his muscles like an antique drapery." The reader blushes for Luther as they both survey the "big green and white club dining room in the sky":

84

Greetings everywhere, and jovial backonings to join this group and that. At the great man's instance, however, they were placed at a table for two, whose outlook seemed to the stranger to embrace the kingdoms of the earth. Life, pulsing life, as far as the embarrassed eye could carry; life in the mazy streets below; life in the forking estuary's tide; life, eager, red-blooded life, to the crest of the horizon's hills! Nerve ganglion of a continent, market-place of a world!

The strength of the author lies primarily in his graphic evocation of the political milieu. The campaign train—whistle stops and all. The whipped-up frenzy of rallies, pianos pounding, banners waving, flares bursting, orators pontificating. The hole-in-the-corner offices from whence the boss sends out his mandates. The social functions in the state capital, at which the inevitable politicking goes on. It is all very bright and brisk, Luther seeming fully at home in the political world.

Something must be said also for his firm tone in denouncing political malfeasance. Refusing to plead in the rather tepid manner of Booth Tarkington, he grimly itemizes the many nineteenth century political vices which continue to appear: the view that civil service is a "damned nuisance," that the party comes foremost,[17] that politicans may have emotions but not convictions, that money to grease the

---

[17] One of the characters in *The Henchman* declares: "Many an unworthy man is worthy of election, even by bribery, because of his party's sake, for that party's success may signify the country's salvation."

A different view from this is proposed by Nick Burr in *The Voice of the People*. Love of honesty is better than love of party, says Nick. But to most people Nick is a "crack-brained moralist."

wheels is essential, that a too nice scrutiny of the means is undesirable if the end is "meet," that nepotism and senatorial courtesy need not go out of fashion.

Edwin E. Slosson at this very time (1906) indicated the importance of such denunciation:

> Fifty years from now, when the historian of American literature writes of the opening of this century, he will give one of his most interesting chapters to the literature of exposure, and he will pronounce it a true intellectual force, a vital element in the creative activities of later years.[18]

This prophecy fails to note the customary lack of a high degree of skill in the fashioning of a political novel such as *The Henchman,* and perhaps makes too much of the form as an "intellectual force," yet it utters a correct prediction as to the novel's being a "vital element" in subsequent years, its aesthetic defects notwithstanding.

[18] Quoted in Louis Filler, *Crusaders for American Liberalism,* 257–58.

CHAPTER VI

In the Vanguard: Churchill and Phillips

THE most representative and probably the best political novelists of the 1900–20 era were Winston Churchill and David Graham Phillips. If not allegorical (like Melville in *Mardi*), nor ideological (like James in *The Princess Casamassima*), these two writers were certainly *political*—using as their prime material the politician at work, portraying the people who influence him, and rehearsing their political actions. The Churchill and Phillips books include descriptions of reformers, bosses and cynical congressmen, attended by a train of "fixers," "boodle-seekers," bribable newspapermen and judges, and operating in legislative halls and smoke-filled hotel rooms. In other words, they "directly describe, interpret or analyze political phenomena."[1] Like the Muckrakers (to which group Phillips most certainly belonged, if Churchill did not), they used the novel as an instrument, to try to gain "a reader's support for a cause, arouse his distaste for a course of action, or simply produce a reevaluation of previously accepted beliefs."[2]

Winston Churchill knew whereof he spoke in dealing with political concerns, having served as a representative in the New Hampshire State Legislature for a number of years,

[1] Joseph Blotner's definition of the political novel. Blotner, *op. cit.*, 2.
[2] *Ibid.*, 10.

having almost been nominated for governor of the state (supposedly, the intervening machinery of the nominating convention, keeping the rank and file of the party from expressing their wishes, prevented his nomination),[3] and having been associated with the national progressive movement as a good friend and supporter of Theodore Roosevelt.

His novels *Coniston* (1906), and *Mr. Crewe's Career* (1908) reflect this background, serving as a picture of boss and corporation rule in the political arena. Always at least partially an historical novelist (as in the best-selling *Richard Carvel* and *The Crossing*), Churchill traces this rule from Jacksonian days down to his own time. In *Coniston* Jethro Bass, tanner in the town of Coniston and a shrewd Yankee type, manages, by buying up mortgages among the farmers— the economic iron hand once again—by doing favors here and there, and by playing upon his opponents' weaknesses with wicked facility, to become the legislative boss of New Hampshire. In *Mr. Crewe's Career* the single boss has given way to a feudal system, with the Northeastern Railway corporation now controlling New Hampshire, the attorney for the railroad, Hilary Vane, directing affairs from behind the scenes at the state capital.

The peculiar force of the novels stems from their realistic presentation of the political scene, an indignant and knowledgeable citizen pointing out the political facts of life. Certain characteristic features stand out. The boss is well defined, his "close to the soil" quality, his "one of the people" approach, as exemplified in Jethro Bass, Bijah Bixby, and Job Braden. Although such men possess loyalty, common

---

[3] Warren I. Titus, *Winston Churchill*, 66.

sense, humor and other desirable attributes, they are primarily motivated by a power drive for self-aggrandizement (complicated, in Bass's case, by a *cherchez la femme* aspect), and the means of advancement cannot be called ethical. Jethro Bass secures votes by not foreclosing mortgages; "Bije" Bixby hands out packets of money in the pre-election season.

The machinations of the corporation, the railroad combine, are also accurately related. Since the corporation, run by President Augustus Flint and Attorney Vane, directs the state legislature, dictates to the Speaker of the House, determines many committee appointments, and creates gubernatorial candidates, the ordinary voter must be regarded as virtually disfranchised.

President Flint attempts to justify corporation rule by stating that the railroad had to enter into politics in order to defend itself from the blackmailing legislators, and he also voices "high-minded" platitudes about conducting the corporation for the benefit of the stockholders. But Churchill takes no stock in this, setting forth the true motive in the question posed by Flint's daughter Victoria: "Isn't it rather the power that is so hard to relinquish?" Feeling that material gratification and selfishness completely replace spiritual values in the big businessmen of his age, Churchill treats Flint (and his forerunner in *Coniston*, Isaac Worthington) more harshly than either the boss or the corporation lawyer.

A favorite nineteenth century type reappears in Churchill's work, the amateur in politics, exemplified by Humphrey Crewe, the rich man who is prepared to employ his leisure—in approved British fashion, says the author—by serving his country. The "gentleman" finds himself on a prickly path, however. His political "education" takes the form of a series of mortifications, dependence on the rural boss Job Braden for nomination, maiden speeches in the legislature marred by rolling cuspidors, idealistic bills smothered in committee, manipulation by the veteran politicos Brush Bascom and Jacob Botcher. Although maintaining his honest course, Mr. Crewe does not succeed in bringing many others to share his principles, and his quest for the governorship is thwarted by the machine. At the end of the book he "is still in politics, and still hopeful," but, asks the reader, with good reason?[4]

Churchill offers other disheartening glimpses of the political scene. In the state legislature the ruling coterie (e.g., the "Honorable" Heth Sutton and Senator Peleg Hartington) keep affairs going as they wish, with the honest farmer representatives so bewildered by the intricacies of parliamentary procedure as to be rendered ineffectual. The Speaker of the House has autocratic power; the governor is a figurehead. Dishonest lawyers and newspapermen do the bidding of the "money men," and, though the average voter knows approximately what is going on, he does little if anything about it.

At the end of each novel an attempt is made by Churchill to relieve the gloom of the picture, in *Coniston* by "retir-

[4] A rather similar portrait of the amateur in politics is offered in a nineteenth century English political novel, George Eliot's *Felix Holt* (1866). Harold Transome, a man of good family, seeks a place in Parliament, feeling duty-bound so to do. Although more aware than Humphrey Crewe of the need for being "practical," yet Transome is "used" by his electioneering agent and involved in campaign measures which he would wish to avoid.

Warren Titus has indicated that Churchill's own experiences in politics in many respects parallel those of Humphrey Crewe (See *ibid.*, 65ff.). If such is the case, one must give the author due credit for being able to laugh at himself.

ing" the boss, in *Mr. Crewe's Career* by declaring that "the era of political domination by a corporation, and mainly for the benefit of a corporation, is over." The reader cannot share the Churchillian belief that boss and corporation power are broken, however. One anticipates successors to Jethro Bass— and indeed, in *Mr. Crewe's Career*, he finds them. The Job Bradens and Brush Bascoms have taken over, and they wield almost as much power as their predecessor.

One is troubled by the resolution of *Coniston's* love story, too, a resolution which effects an undesirable twist in the political plot. In order to bring together the lovers Cynthia Wetherell and Bob Worthington, separated because the former is the ward of Jethro Bass and the latter the son of Bass's political enemy, railroad president Isaac Worthington, Churchill assigns to Bass a final coup, one with devious consequences. Bass musters the vote to defeat a railroad consolidation bill which Worthington is backing and thus holds the whip hand over him, but he surrenders his advantage on condition that Worthington will consent to the marriage of Cynthia and Bob. This is all very well for Cynthia and Bob, but *not* for the state of New Hampshire, for Bass is turning the state over to the railroad power, and the rule of the Worthington forces bodes little good for the public.

Mr. Crewe's Career disappoints at the end, in announcing the cessation of corporation control but not presenting much evidence for this point of view. Although upright individuals like Austen Vane, Victoria Flint, Humphrey Crewe, and Mr. Redbrook exist, and although there is indication that the people would rally behind a candidate for governor of the Austen Vane type, still, the book concludes with Giles Henderson, a tool of the "interests," as the newly elected governor, with the "dirty politics" of the Bascoms and Billings and Dobys and Janes in the forefront, and with the legislature still composed of—in Churchill's heavily ironic phrase—the "noble five hundred of the House and the stanch twenty of the Senate." The "evolution" to something better, of which Austen Vane speaks, seems less inevitable to the reader than to Vane.

As essays in the "art of fiction," *Coniston* and *Mr. Crewe's Career* must be labeled partial successes. In both books Churchill commands almost perpetual attention by virtue of his story-telling flair. Many scenes delight the reader, particularly those with comic overtones like the lively Woodchuck Session, the Jethro Bass-Miss Penniman confrontation in the dress shop, or Humphrey's Crewe's "open house" at Wedderburn. On the other hand, the sentimental passages slow down the pace, as do the plethora of authorial intrusions on the "for a little while we are going to gallop through the years" or "it is certainly not the function of a romance to relate, with the exactness of a House journal, the proceedings of a legislature" order.

A skillful hand at character drawing, Churchill fills the pages of *Coniston* and *Mr. Crewe's Career* with believable creations. One is immediately attracted to *Coniston's* protagonist, Jethro Bass, for the fact that he is "not at first sight a prepossessing-looking person" is counteracted by his evident shrewdness, his sense of humor and general air of sturdiness. His appeal for Cynthia Ware, notwithstanding the vast social gulf between them, is understandable, as his laconic and indirect "courting" is amusing and natural. To

be sure, Jethro must balance off the vices of intense ambition and trickiness against his virtues, but this makes him
all the more real. If his portrait is somewhat weakened at the
end, when sentiment gets the better of the author in outlining the relationship between Bass and his ward Cynthia
Wetherell, the character comes through as a very plausible
"village Yankee."

"Judge" Vane, the central figure in *Mr. Crewe's Career*,
also carries conviction. At first a subscriber to the faith that
railroads rule by "divine right," he modifies his position
gradually, feeling more and more the influence of his ethi-
cally aware son Austen. A dour, lonely individual, one for
whom it is particularly difficult "to give expression to his
feelings," he estranges those closest to him and remains, despite his position of power, alienated and uncomforted until
just before his death.

The sketches of many of the less prominent characters
are also well conceived, feminist Lucretia Penniman, village
types like Lem Hallowell and Moses Hatch, political figures
such as "Ham" Tooting and Adam Hunt. Spinster Euphrasia
Cotton, in *Mr. Crewe's Career*, is an especially interesting version of the tart-tongued but heart-of-gold stereotype, and
the burlesqued title character, Humphrey Crewe, is a pleasant figure of fun. Churchill mocks his social ineptitude, his
naïveté, and his "impenetrable conceit," while at the same
time granting his quickness to learn, his industry, and integrity. One chuckles at Humphrey as he careens around in his
runabout or tactlessly keeps his guests from treading on his
lawn, but one grows to respect his efforts to institute political
reforms.

The novel's quartet of lovers are, it must be admitted, rather shopworn, though the ability of all four to indulge in witty persiflage makes their love passages more bearable. Of the villains, Mr. Worthington and Mr. Flint, less favorable things can be said. The black are simply black.

The author promotes an agreeable realism in his books by means of an authentically etched setting. Rural New England is re-created, the New Hampshire hill country of spread-out villages, boulder-strewn pastures, and wooded tracts. Jabe Jenny's farmhouse, white, with great trees and an old-fashioned flower garden surrounding, lilacs clustering about the small-paned windows and bittersweet clinging to the roof, stands, like many another, as a beautifully simple adornment to the landscape.

The down-to-earth humor coursing through the novels cuts the sentiment and occasional pomposity and also contributes to the realism. The conversational exchange between the pretentious Mrs. Pomfret and the taciturn Job Braden amusingly captures their diametrically opposed natures. The "biter bit" sequences, those in which Jethro Bass outsmarts the Worthington-Duncan group by securing a postmaster-ship from President Grant through an adroitly arranged interview, or his defeat of the Duncans and Lovejoys by luring them to a theater performance and away from a vital legislative session, stir the reader to laughter, as do the bits of good-humored satire ("one felt that Mr. Flint's handshake was not an absolute gift of his soul").

For the most part Churchill writes with a natural ease, whether calling attention to "an elderly man of comfortable proportions . . . who gave, somehow, the polished impression

94

of a marble," or reproducing the country dialect so replete with "I callate's" and "drat it's," "wahn't" and "acrost," or making use of a homely figure of speech ("he was merely puzzled as a June-bug is puzzled when it bumps up against a wire windowscreen"). He relies rather infrequently on image patterns, though fond of outlining political maneuvers in terms of the military and though suggesting the tightness of the political hierarchy by mocking employment of feudal terminology—fiefs and vassals, chamberlains and seneschals. If he intersperses a shade too much rhetoric—"well-remembered scene!" / "woe to the Honorable Adam B. Hunt!"—with the homespun, and even inserts some sugary verses, Churchill still manages to convey a sense of professionalism, at least when compared with so many of his "journalistic" contemporaries.

The most productive of these contemporaries was David Graham Phillips, who, in the brief span of ten years,[5] turned out, as one facet of his muckraking endeavors, several political or semipolitical novels. Whether fictionalizing on the subject of "made marriages," or rampant capitalism, or chicanery in the life insurance industry, Phillips invariably served up the theme of the *People* versus *Privilege* and invariably set forth the political implications in this contest.

His first novel, *The Great God Success* (1901), depicts the efforts of a newspaper editor to expose political corruption and to plead for the restoration of government to the populace. Successful at first in unveiling legislative evils and

---

[5] In this short period, Phillips—writing from 11:00 P.M. to 6:00 A.M. seven days a week—managed to produce twenty-five books and hundreds of articles. See Kenneth S. Lynn, *The Dream of Success*, 127.

in "showing up" professed reformers, the editor suddenly switches his position when he is bribed with an ambassadorial post by the business interests, and thus political victory is snatched from the people after all. Phillips, as he is wont to do, simplifies the issues, makes the editor's turnabout far too abrupt, and certainly stretches credulity in allowing a national election to hinge upon one man's reversal. In so doing, he unfortunately invalidates his "message."

Golden Fleece (1903), devoted to expressing the author's disgust at the current popular practice of marrying off the daughters of the American plutocracy to European noblemen, is less politically oriented, in fact, touches upon political matters scarcely at all. It does register one of Phillips' favorite political convictions, however, the firm belief that money rules in this area as in so many others. The example of Senator Pope, a nonentity who has achieved his position only by virtue of his generous financial support of his party, gives credence to Phillips' contention.

The Cost (1904) embroiders upon this theme, rehearsing the political machinations engaged in by the men-with-the-money. The mighty and menacing plutocracy, embodied here in the Woolen Trust headed by John Dumont, invades politics to protect its power. In the face of this invasion, the people, "prosperous and therefore quiescent," at first appear unconcerned. When a magnetic, reform-minded lawyer, Hampden Scarborough, stirs them up, however, they enthusiastically place him in the governor's chair and anticipate his breaking the sway of the corporations. After his election, though, Scarborough vanishes from the story.[6] Phillips there-

[6] He returns at the end of the novel to marry his one true love, the

after returns to John Dumont and concentrates on the Wall Street economic battle. Both the people and the people's champion are forgotten!

The most truly political novels in this fictional flurry of Phillips are *The Plum Tree* (1905), *Joshua Craig* (1909), and *George Helm* (1912).[7] The former follows the career of Midwesterner Harvey Sayler, who climbs the political ladder deftly, if unethically, not worrying very much about the means used to advance himself. His end is good, however, a desire to checkmate the Eastern stock market crowd and to enhance the welfare of the people. Although a practical politician, who acts as the custodian of the "plum tree," distributing favors as necessary, directing campaigns, making and breaking individuals, Sayler, by virtue of retaining the "handicap of idealism," commands far more respect than either corporation president Roebuck or Senators Dunkirk and Goodrich. He does not, of course, stand as high as Hampden Scarborough. The erstwhile governor of *The Cost* ascends to

widow of John Dumont. He also returns in Phillips' next novel, *The Plum Tree*.

Grant Knight suggests that Phillips had his old friend Albert J. Beveridge, the Progressive senator from Indiana, in mind in creating the character of Scarborough. The political novel would seem to function once again as a *roman à clef*. Knight also equates President Burbank, in *The Plum Tree*, with McKinley, and Harvey Sayler with Mark Hanna. Mary Dillon's "leader," in *The Leader*, he says may be Bryan; I. K. Friedman's "radical," in *The Radical*, may be Senator Bruce McAllister. See Grant C. Knight, *The Strenuous Age in American Literature*, 170. According to Warren Titus, Churchill's Jethro Bass is modeled on Ruel Durkee, the rural boss of New Hampshire (Titus, *op. cit.*, 67).

[7] Tangentially political are two other novels, *The Deluge* (1905) and *Light-Fingered Gentry* (1907). These resemble *The Cost* in attributing political intervention to the "rascals of high finance," the motive again being self-protection.

97

the Presidency in *The Plum Tree*, and there he will function, so Phillips assures us, as a "President without fear or favor . . . he will really obey the Constitution, will really enforce the laws!" Phillips establishes in Scarborough what Kenneth Lynn calls a Messiah-Lochinvar archetype—a very romanticized image![8]

The hero of *Joshua Craig* is another Messiah-Lochinvar from the Middle West, storming, like Scarborough, into Washington to purify the scene. Joshua is also concerned about the masses and basically more honest than most of those whom he encounters in the national capital. But he is by no means as perfect a "democrat" as Scarborough and does not escape the corrupting Washington atmosphere.

The Messiah-Lochinvar protagonist of Phillips' final novel, *George Helm*, more precisely mirrors the Scarborough type. George Helm also progresses rapidly from small-town "lawyering" to a governorship and on a similar protect-the-people platform. During his term of office he refuses to be manipulated by politicians like "Boss" Sayler or by his father-in-law, lumber "king" George Clearwater, but this very independence—so he informs his wife at the conclusion of the novel—will no doubt prevent his re-election. If there were a real "people," intelligent, persistent, not easily fooled, the reformers like Scarborough and himself might linger in office. But the people are "conquerable and easy to rob and oppress"; privilege still has the upper hand.

Novels such as these three seem, alas, "programmatically barren."[9] The reader does not share Phillips' faith in the

[8] Lynn, *op. cit.*, 139ff.
[9] *Ibid.*, 148.

Messiah-Lochinvar figure, first, because the figure is too idealized, secondly, because his accomplishments in office are very lightly sketched in. About Scarborough we learn only that he "went after the monopolies," about Helm, that he enforced inspection of beer production and made the railroads pay taxes, about Craig, nothing. All three, as mellifluous orators, inspire "spasms of virtue" in the body politic but fail to achieve many concrete or lasting reforms.

If Phillips could not advance many positive suggestions as to how to restrain big business and to "alert" the people permanently, he did give evidence of possessing considerable political "savvy." The "backstage" glimpses in *The Plum Tree*—of Senator Sayler arranging for the passage of "black bills," or concocting a "pilgrimage plan" for presidential candidate Burbank (derived from McKinley's "front porch" campaign?), or outsmarting the "Wall Street whales"—have an indisputably veracious air, and, similarly, the talk in *George Helm* about "sacrificial candidates," "social bribes," and "machine nominations." As B. O. Flower said of *The Plum Tree*, and might have said of *George Helm*, "It unmasks present political conditions in a manner so graphic, so convincing, and so compelling that it cannot fail to arouse. . . ."[10]

Judged as works of art rather than as political documents, the Phillips novels do not inspire much enthusiasm. One may credit the author with sheer narrative power, an

---

[10] Quoted in Roy P. Fairfield, "Benjamin Orange Flower: Father of the Muckrakers," *American Literature*, Vol. 22 (November, 1950), 280.

Joshua Craig must be counted out here, for it is almost entirely given over to the protagonist as a lover, treating him as a congressman in very fleeting fashion.

ability to move his tale along easily, and sometimes excitingly (e.g., the scene between Madam Bowker and Congressman Craig in *Joshua Craig*), and one occasionally encounters an arresting characterization, such as that of Margaret Severance or Harvey Sayler, but Phillips' performance, taken as a whole, is distressingly uneven.

Let us take the matter of character drawing. In "Boss" Sayler, Phillips presents an interestingly complex individual. So strong and Machiavellian that his wife both fears and distrusts him, Sayler yet recognizes the ruthlessness of his political career and is not without qualms at its cost ("within me . . . a dual personality: . . . one that does, and another that watches"). His quick wit and sensitivity, his "genial philosophy of mingled generosity and cynicism" intrigue the reader, who sees in him a very human mixture of positive and negative qualities.

On the other hand, a character like Joshua Craig seems badly drawn. Not that he is too much whitened (like Governor Scarborough), nor too much blackened (like Senator Dunkirk), but rather that the author and the reader entertain such disparate views about him. Intending his "hero" to be admirable, Phillips succeeds only in making him "one of the leading boors in American literature."[11] Conceited, vain, insulting, patronizing, Joshua Craig strikes one as a veritable bounder, hardly as a *savior* figure. Bemused by his worship of the local-Midwestern-boy-makes-good legend, Phillips does not conceive his character clearly and ends with a highly ambiguous creation.

Phillips handles many of the technical problems in his

[11] Lynn, *op. cit.*, 145.

fiction in a rather slipshod way. The discursiveness of his structure, for example, is suggested by his habit of allowing characters to drop out of his story for long intervals, then suddenly reappear, only to vanish again. The third person omniscient point of view, which he customarily employs, permits him to overindulge in authorial intrusion. We must bear with editorializing passages, sententious observations, and slanted statements ("A *man* had come to town"), all of them making us feel too "manipulated." The one novel (*The Plum Tree*) which utilizes a first rather than third person narrator avoids this sense of manipulation (the reader is naturally drawn to the narrator and accepts his story as authentic), and makes one wish that Phillips had chosen the autobiographical method more often.

An absence of "settings" flaws many of the novels, one hardly sensing the Middle Western town from which the Phillips heroes spring, nor the Washington environment to which they transplant themselves. Those two vices of the second-rate novel, melodrama and sentimentality, are, on the other hand, only too much present. The Granby hanging and the recounting of "Doc" Woodruff's checkered past in *The Plum Tree*, or the final description in *The Cost* of financier Dumont dead amidst tangles of ticker tape, exemplify the former; and the scenes between Harvey Sayler and his mother, or between Sayler and Elizabeth Crosby in *The Plum Tree*, the latter. When women are involved, Phillips is apt to become exceedingly sloppy.

Startlingly juxtaposed to the saccharine passages (e.g., "a man would hesitate to kiss her unless he were well shaved") are many realistic ones. Often Phillips writes most frankly, assigning "shabby, shamed" clothes to his rough-hewn heroes, allowing a dinner party of "first citizens" to descend into a "repulsive mass of unmasked, half-drunken, wholly infuriated brutes," flatly asserting that, as the social system is arranged in America, "woman has little to think about but men." The political sections of the novels become decidedly sordid, as the author, scoffing at the notion that politics can be honest in a society where men live by taking advantage of one another, impartially fires away at both the masses and their bosses.

The Phillips style is brightened now and then by some much-in-little phrasing. The Stillwater girls are neatly summarized as "hastily made-over Westerners." Josh Craig's exuberance is captured in the comment that his "arrivals were always swoopings." Governor Burbank's perfunctory grief at the death of his wife is indicated in the remark that, "after a few of those stereotyped mortuary sentences, he shifted to politics." Of a "diplomatic invitation" Phillips tartly says, ". . . it sounded cordial, yet—was safely vague." The successful politician is summed up as "keen, cynical, indifferent." In every case the satiric implications are sharpened by the succinctness.

Beyond praise of such concision and of a natural use of idiomatic and dialectal language (Phillips depends heavily on dialogue), one is not able to go, however; the author's style, judged as a whole, reveals far more defects than virtues. Much of the figurative language is colorless or trite ("black cave of despair," "vexed political ocean"). Imagery is sparsely used, and, when brought into play, may be too heavily insisted upon. Phillips' "plum tree" metaphor, appropriate though it may be, recurs too often. Overwriting prevails in many a passage—beards as "carmine masks," protagonists "flashing with manliness"—and a transparently rhetorical tone sets the reader's teeth on edge. Awkward grammar ("There is always a lot of fellows . . .") and ponderous constructions ("as soon as Dufour had taken his heavy body away . . ."), unhappy word choice ("he had small and wanting confidence"), and cacophonous expressions ("gapes up at the great with glamoured eyes") strike one as sloppily journalistic and push Phillips some leagues away from literary artistry.

One may still conclude that Churchill and Phillips were the best of their time, their literary standards surpassing those of their contemporaries (Phillips's just barely!), and their commentary on turn-of-the-century politics being authoritative. One regrets, however, that in their readiness to regard the novel as a political instrument, they failed to make full use of the "alchemy of art."

☆

CHAPTER VII

The Campaign Continued (1920-1964)

A S our study moves into the present era, we discover that the political novelist is still intent upon castigating various abuses on the American political front, carping at the boss, the lobbyist, and the weak-kneed congressman, and bemoaning the worship of the gospel of the "larger good" (*i.e.*, any means to the end). In fact, the thing that most impresses one as he reads current or very recent fiction of this type is the sameness of the genre. The monotony of the argument in the political novel from the Gilded Age on was noted not long ago by Henry Steele Commager—an apt notation, though the comment Commager added, ". . . politics was thought worthy of literary treatment only when ostentatiously unworthy,"[1] was less accurate. Books such as *All the King's Men* and *The Last Hurrah* tend to refute such a charge, apologizing as they do for some "unworthy" politics by explaining how good can emerge from evil practices.

However, the monotony of which Commager speaks is indeed evident—mostly in the fact that the people and institutions subjected to attack have changed little, nor have the methods of the attackers. The most recent crop of political novelists (fewer in number than the muckrakers, but just

[1] Henry Steele Commager, *The American Mind*, 62.

104

as fervent) concentrate on the topics introduced by their predecessors and go on record as sharing the earlier belief that the old integrities are *still* disintegrating in the face of a complex political, social, and economic order, and that something must be done.

Although corruption in government remains the favorite subject, several modern writers have become concerned with a different aspect of politics, with its theory and ideological content, and thus branch out in a new direction, new in American political fiction, that is.[2] In particular, they have chosen to deal with the threat posed by international Communism. One sees many manifestations: John Steinbeck on the party organizer, Sinclair Lewis on Fascism, John Dos Passos on domestic and Ernest Hemingway on international Communism, and Irwin Shaw on McCarthyism.

This interest in political *ideas* has introduced greater complexity and intellectual fluidity into the political novel, and when these are combined with more insight into individual motivation and behavior (as in Lionel Trilling's study of the liberal in *The Middle of the Journey*), the form acquires more vitality. Although it retains a sameness—"a continuity in the phenomena and ideas it treats," as Joseph

---

[2] European novels, the work of writers like Stendhal, Dostoevski, Disraeli, and Eliot have usually concentrated on political theory as the basis for their drama.

They did not entirely avoid the subject of corruption, however. Witness George Eliot's Felix Holt wondering what was the use of pulling at the tangled skein of electioneering trickery. "As long as three-fourths of the men in this country see nothing in an election but self-interest, and nothing in self-interest but some form of greed, one might as well try to purify the proceedings of the fishes." George Eliot, *Felix Holt*, (Boston, Little, Brown, and Company, 1900), 169–70.

Blotner puts it[3]—yet it shows the possibilities of expansion while at the same time remaining a lively genre.

Since the "liveliness" is often derived from the fiction's background, the political setting of the age, it behooves us to examine briefly the history of the period stretching from 1920 to the present. Twentieth century political novelists usually resort, as had their forerunners, to their own times for material.[4]

The modern era is marked by continued political turbulency, and hence the novelists find a plethora of controversial subjects with which to deal. Although most historians would say that, on the whole, political morality has improved in the present century, yet the corruption in high places in the Harding regime equalled that of the Reconstruction era, the New Deal decade was not devoid of shoddiness (at least, according to John Dos Passos), and the 1940's and 1950's have displayed some government-by-crony characteristics and some unattractive dealings in mink coats and the like.[5] If reforms in municipal government and in the civil service have gone steadily on, nonetheless, abuses continue to appear, as recent novels such as Martin Mayer's *Governor's Choice* (1956), William Brammer's *The Gay Place* (1961), Henry J. Taylor's *The Big Man* (1964), and James D. Horan's

---

[3] Blotner, *op. cit.*, 94.

[4] A few historical novels on political topics continue to appear, e.g., Bellamy Partridge's *Big Freeze* (1948) and James Ford's *Hot Corn Ike* (1923).

[5] Recent histories, such as Karl E. Meyer's *The New America, Politics and Society in the Age of the Smooth Deal*, Blair Bolles' *Men of Good Intentions: Crisis of the American Presidency*, and George A. Graham's *Morality in American Politics* testify that political scandals still abound.

The Seat of Power (1965) are quick to point out. A cyclical pattern of corruption, revulsion, and reform is repeated ad infinitum.

In the 1920's Jazz Age, America's "business civilization" gaily flourished—at least, until 1929. The robber barons modern version—less piratical and highhanded and more often corporation-bound—existed, but these moguls, the Insulls and Van Sweringens, were less active in governmental affairs than their predecessors had been. The really new and powerful plutocrats of the 1920's turned out to be the gangsters and racketeers, and it was they who did most of the tampering with politics. Corrupting public authority for their own ends, they set up vast industrial combinations, organized their own distributive outlets, established their own "impartial arbiters."[6]

Al Capone, for example, ruled in Chicago, Dutch Schultz (protected by the political power of Jimmy Hines) in New York. "Decay's effacing finger" appeared everywhere, in the gambling houses, narcotics trade, illegal liquor traffic, industrial rackets, night clubs, and numbers games. The "new" plutocracy, to be sure, did feel it necessary to be careful of public opinion. Whereas the Morgans and Vanderbilts had dared to say, "I owe the public nothing," or "the public be damned," the Capones and Schultzes, though engaged in only slightly more nefarious undertakings, were not so blithely accepted by the people and consequently had to be more circumspect.

A period of agitation, in short, the 1920's. It was "distinguished" by the Palmer raids on "anarchists," by Ku

[6] Lloyd Morris, *Postscript to Yesterday*, 65.

Klux Klan exposés, by the scandals attached to the administration of "good companion" Harding. The multiple disturbances of the period—shoddy real estate booms in Florida, the Scopes trial in Tennessee, the Sacco-Vanzetti case in Massachusetts—seemed to reach a disastrous climax in the stock market crash.

When the "angry thirties" were ushered in, American life acquired a darker complexion. Although some people, even in the breadline days of the depression, were willing to believe that prosperity was just around the corner, the majority of Americans felt less optimistic. Searching for solutions to the economic woes that beset the country, they endorsed technocracy, Communism, southern agrarianism, and many another sure-fire cure. One of the most vocal of the groups, the "Marxists," seized the opportunity offered by the national discontent to attempt to lead the workers and impoverished farmers into a classic "revolution." But the United States was not so disposed, even in the worst of "hard times."[7]

More influential than the Marxists, or the Technocrats, the Southern Agrarians, or the Social Gospel-ites were the New Dealers led by Franklin D. Roosevelt. Sensing the need, in that time of crisis, for preserving "American capitalism by invoking the positive power of the national government to support and stabilize the economy,"[8] the New Dealers

[7] If the Marxists failed in their major aim, they did achieve lesser goals, however—and mostly commendable goals these were, a successful fight for the rights of minorities and a dramatization of unemployment. Much of the word "Communist" then meant, as Ruth Chatterton said in her political novel *The Betrayers* (1953), "caring for people."

[8] Clinton Rossiter, *The American Presidency*, 210.

concentrated on central government planning. In so doing, they sought to bring relief to the country in the quickest way; they did not intend, as so many of their fellow citizens chose to suspect, to lead the nation down the road to socialism, and certainly not to dictatorship. If many errors were committed in the process of centralization (the flock of alphabetical agencies descending upon Washington seemed bound to promote a bureaucratic tangle), still, the Roosevelt regime did pull America out of the depression.

Whatever one's view on the still sore subject of the New Deal[9] and of F.D.R.—although he could say "My old friend" in eleven languages, he by no means endeared himself to all —one must agree with the general concensus that the ten years proved troubling all the way through. After the economic balance was somewhat righted, upsetting international events such as the Moscow Trials, the Spanish Civil War, the German territorial acquisitions came along to jar the more thoughtful Americans. The nation was also upset by affairs closer to home, the Supreme Court fight of 1937, revivals of anti-Semitism and of racketeering, the presence on the scene of native fascists like Father Coughlin and Gerald L. K. Smith, and at the close of the decade the conflict between America Firsters and interventionists. The "fireside chats" of President Roosevelt and the "gangbusters" of J. Edgar Hoover failed to bring any great degree of comfort.

During the war years of the early 40's, one might observe a united country, and in the last half of that decade

---

[9] Richard Hofstadter reminds us that "The New Deal will never be understood by anyone who looks for a single thread of policy." Hofstadter, *op. cit.*, 331–32.

one might observe a prosperous country as well, the impetus of war production, having carried over into the peacetime period. Yet much industrial strife was in evidence, even though the era of the malefactors of great wealth had clearly ended, thanks to the Securities Exchange Act and other ethical restraints upon wild speculation. Political chicanery still existed, however, despite such legislation as the Hatch Act of 1940 to limit campaign expenditures and contributions. There were many ways of getting around this, as Jim Farley and others quickly discovered. The professional politicians still ran the show, and only a few could be labeled untainted.

Lobbyists of all kinds inundated the national capital, members of permanent organizations, "influence" lawyers, or those operating in social circles. These members of the "third house" busily sought jobs or diplomatic posts or protection for the business interests, bringing unethical pressure to bear. The "boss" still flourished, too, Pendergast in Kansas City, Hague in Jersey City, Edward J. Flynn in the Bronx. In 1947 the Bronx leader published a book, *You're the Boss*, cheerily defending the political machine and bossism in the large cities. Flynn envisioned honest bosses—no gangsters allowed —carefully organizing their parties, but insisted that power still rested in the hands of the people ("you're the boss") and suggested that tidier politics would not result until many men and women "grubbed around" in the political arena.

An unsettled spirit continued to prevail in the 1950's. International unease of course posed the greatest threat to security, a threat constantly maintained by the unpredictable diplomacy of the Russians, by the long-continuing debate over suspension of nuclear bomb testing, and by the Red scare of the first years of the decade. The latter event, as manifested in McCarthyism, has provoked more than one political novelist into an outburst, writers such as Ruth Chatterton, Irwin Shaw, and William L. Shirer having aired their views on the extravagances of the extreme anti-Communists.

Discontent has arisen, too, from the existence of such problems—even in the age of the "Fair Deal"—as juvenile delinquency, TV quiz scandals, and the seemingly admired antics of shoddy café society. The overwhelming prosperity which has come to most Americans, with a resulting "conspicuous consumption" and "conspicuous waste," has also caused some qualms of conscience.

Money still tampers with politics, too, and the Truman era Thomas-Caudle-Vaughan favor doers have their counterpart in the Goldfine-Adams nexus in Eisenhower's administration, and perhaps in the Bobby Bakers of Johnson's. If this most recent decade offers nothing to compare with the scandal-ridden Harding regime, still, the presence of subversives in government, and of Hoffas in labor does not permit a feeling of satisfaction as one views the national scene. Even the New Frontier reflects a pattern of "unbroken tension, repeated crises, and prolonged stalemate in the omnipresent cold war."[10]

Most of the political novels of the last forty years contain angry accounts of the political operations of these years, singling out various features for derision or contempt. Searing comment on political degradation rather than speculative comment on political doctrine continues to be the prevailing pattern.

[10] Link, *op. cit.*, 857.

An initial object of concern for the generally hostile novelist is the Washington politician. This figure holds the center of the stage, for example, in a novel like Samuel Adams' *Revelry* (1926) or Francis Hackett's *The Senator's Last Night* (1943). The former gives a no-holds-barred fictional account of the Harding administration, depicting an easygoing, inconsequential President, surrounded by his shabby circle of advisors and fellow poker players. The real power in the government is Dan Lurcock, one holding simply a nominal position in the attorney-general's office, yet one who steers the epileptic attorney-general *and* the President around at will. The real cabinet includes, says Adams in not very subtle satiric terms, the secretary of deals, secretary of pardons, and the bootlegger general. One of the President's chief cronies, Handy-Andy Gandy, secures a new cabinet post, that of public health, and by virtue of extensive graft in hospital supplies makes a very good thing of it indeed. Meanwhile, the other "cronies" profit in oil deals and the like.

Adams gives to the President some virtues, including that of considerable personal charm and of loyalty. But the latter turns into a weakness, since the President carries it too far, both with regard to his political party (the party is always right; much misdoing may be countenanced on the grounds of its being good for the party), and with regard to his friends. He is so fanatically loyal to his friends that he overlooks their wrongdoing, and thus becomes a tool for grafters, deadbeats, and incompetents. The President himself Adams savagely indicts as unprincipled, hypocritical, mountebankish, immoral, narrow (he shows no interest in foreign affairs), and so on and on. Unsparingly the author lashes the Harding era,

112

revealing its maladministration and corruption. One believes in his graphic assault, though wishing it might have been less ponderously rendered.

Washington appears no more attractive in *The Senator's Last Night,* being filled with political figures like the reactionary isolationist Senator Copley and the more literate and intelligent but equally unscrupulous Senator Sargent. "Rugged Power" is frankly their god, and the survival of the fittest principle prevails. An "invisible government," unconcerned about the people (who are "worth only what they'll bring in the market") rules in a cold and sterile fashion.

Thomas S. Stribling's *The Sound Wagon* (1935) also describes the "rat-race" in the national capital. When Representative Caridius arrives in the city, he is first initiated into Congressional ways by Congressman Bing, who teaches him for one thing, how to make a profit out of one's mileage allowance. This marks the beginning of the fledgling representative's discoveries about life on Capitol Hill. He subsequently learns that congressmen really concern themselves only with appropriations or legislation affecting their district's interests; that in Washington as elsewhere one must know the right people; that Congress is a trading post, the members swapping votes, but no one voting for the interests of the country at large; that lobbyists are omnipresent; and that nepotism plays a featured role (this is carried to such an extreme that sometimes the relatives on a congressman's staff draw money without ever gracing Washington with their presence). Much cause for cynicism here.

When Caridius goes on to the Senate from the House of Representatives—after spending money lavishly in his campaign and vilifying his opponent ruthlessly—he encounters similar conditions. Completely succumbing to his environment, he engages in all the accepted practices and achieves success—until he is tripped up in a peculiarly blatant case of vote buying. Although landing in jail, he is not overly disturbed, for he finds it a rather comfortable "political club," with many cabinet members and congressmen in attendance. Moreover, he expects, after serving his year term, to return to politics more popular than ever, having acquired a "sentimental grip" on the people. Lest one regard author Stribling as exaggerating here, he has only to recall that Boston's James M. Curley, on his return from a year in Danbury prison, was given a most tumultuous reception in the South Station by his "sentimentally gripped" supporters and was able to continue his political career, his popularity enhanced rather than diminished.

Many political novelists devote their attention to state officials rather than Washington politicos, usually choosing, as do William R. Burnett in *King Cole* (1936) and Martin Mayer in *Governor's Choice* (1956), the "chief" of the state, the governor, or else some key behind-the-scenes figure, as is Paul Wellman's practice in *The Walls of Jericho* (1938) and Eugene Burdick's in *The Ninth Wave* (1956).

Burnett's book outlines the rapid political rise of "King Cole" in Ohio. Ambitious and egotistic but also intelligent and clever, Cole knows, and does not hesitate to use, all the political tricks. He is supported by some smooth-working party machinery directed by manager Sullivan and is supplied with the necessary "moola" by the reactionary "money men" in the state. They put down the rival candidacy of honest visionary Asa Fielding, not hesitating to resort to "blackshirt" tactics and damaging "Red" smear labels in the process. In his drive for power Cole will employ any means to the end. He is at least honest with himself, recognizing that the politician is little more than a confidence man bent upon taking in the public, the "suckers." Burnett's picture of the man of *some* good will, perverted by the political life, with its trickery, selfishness, and changes of front, has been standard since the 1890's.

Two decades later, in *Governor's Choice*, the picture has still not changed. "Billy" Clelland, governor of a middle western state, is handsome, ambitious, intelligent, relatively honest, and successful, but he studiously "plays the game" in order to achieve success. Whether diligently attending the state university football games or investigating some much publicized gambling scandals, he is always doing the 'politic' thing, that which will contribute to the furthering of his ambitions. Although no one would declare that to be ambitious is undesirable, the power complex can corrode, and so it does with Governor Clelland.

Like King Cole he comes to believe that the means can be dishonest to arrive at honest ends. One needs principles, yes, but also "perspective" and "proportion." Even when, in the book's crucial final scene, he makes a "governor's choice" which would seem to be based on principle alone, the author does not allow us to be sure of his motives and does make clear that the decision will work to Clelland's political advantage. No one's hands stay very clean in politics. How could they when a malicious press hounds the politician, when gangster elements attempt to muscle in, and when the state and county machines manipulate political affairs? The combination of an unhealthy environment and of intense personal ambition proves Clelland's undoing.

Paul Wellman's *The Walls of Jericho* reproduces the common image of politics as dirty, sordid, and corrupt, while resuming the favorite argument of the late nineteenth century political novelists that an oligarchy of businessmen directs legislative processes. The representative figure is businessman Porter Grimes, controlling politics in this instance in Kansas, just as his counterparts control them elsewhere throughout the country. Although facing opposition here, from both the honest insurgent type Dave Constable and from the dishonest schemer Judge Hutto, Grimes in general has his way. At least, that for which he stands, money and influence, take precedence over human rights. The curse of American politics, states author Wellman, is the politician, playing a game "in which scruples are only a weakness," and for which the people in the end must pay.

Utterly unscrupulous certainly is the "hero" of *The Ninth Wave*, Mike Freesmith, a lawyer engaged—in the latter half of the novel—in securing the California governorship for his law partner John Cromwell. Freesmith is presented by author Burdick as a study of the ill effects of a power complex. From youth onward, Freesmith based his life on a few harsh principles: the tough people get ahead, the masses love a man who humbles them, the masses yield to the authority who can satisfy their fundamental desires to hate and to fear, the masses are so many "lemmings."

Himself one of the "tough people," Freesmith becomes a merciless authoritarian, finding scope for his ambition in an attempt to steer Cromwell into the governorship and to boss California politics generally. He works hardest in the preprimary convention, where there are only five hundred people, the delegates, to influence—or, to put it in his terms, to "scare." By stirring up fear and hate, he secures the en-dorsement of the "oldsters" (a large group in California) and the support of Notestein, political agent of the public utility, and of the oil companies, and thus secure the convention nomination and bestows it on Cromwell.

In the ensuing campaign Freesmith concentrates on the undecided 10 per cent of the voters. The 45 per cent who will vote Republican infallibly (for all kinds of silly rea-sons) and the 45 per cent who will vote Democratic infallibly (for all kinds of silly reasons) he ignores. Working on his fear and hatred principle, he indulges in a successful whisper-ing campaign against the opposition candidate and, by in-timidation tactics, swings the moneyed people behind Crom-well. But the election does not fall to Cromwell after all, for Mike is drowned just before the voting, and Cromwell, free from his influence, deliberately jettisons the blackmail methods and also recants on some Communist-smear de-vices he had previously used.

Mike is drowned by his best friend, Hank Moore, acting on the necessity of negating Mike's philosophy. He refuses to believe that the people are always scared, always fearful, agreeing, one assumes, with Cromwell's description: "They're stupid, frightened, panic-stricken. But they're also wise, cour-ageous, steady." Hank Moore has done right, according to Burdick, in refuting the theory of mass irrationality, though he will suffer as the "murderer" (the implication is made,

117

however, that Freesmith could have broken out of Hank's grip) of his friend.

In a sense the political background of *The Ninth Wave* is incidental. Freesmith's authoritarian personality and cynicism with regard to the masses could have been explored in other settings. But the background is convincingly suggested, more so than the "foreground" really. Mike Freesmith, inhuman in his calculations with regard to people and "abstracted" throughout, takes on a "stagey" quality. The "ninth wave"—the biggest, and hence a power symbol—which he rides so deftly almost swamps him, after all, in making him seem a larger-than-life-figure, and very unreal. In the last analysis, the "debris of politics" is more firmly rendered than the study of power.

Judging from the work of other political novelists, the "debris" exists in city as well as in state government. The early pages of Stribling's *The Sound Wagon*, for example, have a city setting and reflect a dismal scene. Lawyer Caridius appears initially as an honest candidate for Congress, the choice of the Independent Voters' Alliance and pledged to oppose corruption. But he soon encounters obstacles such as a ruling city ring, indifferent voters, and powerful corporations, and the whole paraphernalia of "practical politics." That is, the candidate says one thing to strikebreakers inside the plant, quite another thing to strikers outside, and he offers as his formal reason for seeking office an independent candidacy indebted to neither major party and serving the majority of the people, although his real hope is to make a good enough showing so that one or the other of the major parties will take him up. The "independence" lasts only until then.

Caridius secures his office through the agency of the political boss Big Stick Krauseman and by obtaining the "repeater" votes of Andy Blank's supporters. He quickly becomes involved with people like Canarelli, a gangster who controls most of the city's rackets (and is worried when elections come about for fear he will have to buy a new set of cops and judges); lawyer Myerberg, who scorns "reformers"; financier Littenham, a behind-the-scenes political power; and various servile editors in the pay of Littenham and with no sense of responsibility to the public.

Caridius' city is underworld-controlled, boss Krauseman acting as a go-between for the financial and criminal interests, preserving the democratic government in form only. Canarelli pays off state and city officials and is disturbed because he cannot pay off the federal ones too ("I need a senator of my own"). The underworld and local bosses own the city and the state; the banks and corporations own the federal government. Stribling includes all levels in his corrosive survey.

As the appearance of Big Stick Krauseman in *The Sound Wagon* suggests, the "boss" lingers on in the political novel. One may cite Joseph Dinneen's *Ward Eight* (1936), Henry Clune's *By His Own Hand* (1952), Harry Sylvester's *Moon Gaffney* (1947), and Edwin O'Connor's *The Last Hurrah* (1956) among others. Dinneen's book, historical rather than topical, goes back to turn-of-the-century Boston to describe the career of ward boss Hughie Donnelly. Hughie controls

Ward Eight, a large and crucial (in elections) district, made up at first of the Irish, later the Italian immigrants. Hughie's henchmen take the immigrants in hand—they are voters, after all—the minute they land, providing jobs and places to live, and securing their everlasting gratitude and constant support.

Hughie, backed by his loyal voter core and his loyal workers, rules with an iron hand, handpicking delegates to party caucuses, and disseminating instructions through his "kitchen cabinet." He knows so precisely how much of the vote he can deliver (not only the Irish, but the Italian as well, since he has secured the discipleship of Tony DiPisa) that he can predict the outcome of elections with certainty. Thus everything hinges upon him. On the one occasion when matters do get out of hand and an honest business government takes over, Hughie sits back unconcerned, knowing that he will be returned to his place in power, the people being more at home with the grafters, and better off, too. Hughie, Dinneen would have us remember, does perform kindnesses, is a man of his word, and "honest according to his code."

Sylvester's *Moon Gaffney* updates the era and shifts the setting to New York City but otherwise provides little change. The tight organization of ward bosses and district captains, of mayors as front men, and of the city hall hierarchy is outlined, and the constant political maneuvering— at union meetings, dances, even wakes—as well. Sylvester does add a new element in introducing some ideological discussion, but this takes the rather rudimentary form of anti-Jewish, anti-Negro, and anti-Communist tirades.

Henry Clune follows the lead of Dinneen in drawing a

rather flattering portrait of the boss in his book *By His Own Hand*, as does also Edwin O'Connor in *The Last Hurrah*.[11] Most of the present-day novels appear to lack the savage thrust of those of earlier eras like Flower's *The Spoilsmen* or Shapley's *Solid For Mulhooly*. Perhaps this is owing to the disappearance of the vicious big-city boss of the Tweed type. O'Connor's genial modern model, Frank Skeffington seems but a distant cousin of Tammany Hall's Barton Seacrist.

One other governmental level, what we might call grassroots politics, occupies the attention of some modern political novelists. It is, for example, the province of McCready Huston in *Dear Senator* (1928). Huston follows the career of "Dan" (his real name is Scott, but this would never do in politics) Meredith, a United States senator, but one whom we see in action not in Washington, but in his own state and county. A shrewd and unscrupulous demagogue—the stereotype again—Meredith deftly climbs into power, speechifying (he has the knack of making platitudes sound like forceful logic), winning the favor of the Republican county boss, Seneca Giles, and making various "arrangements" until he is able to say, "I'm a senator." Unfortunately, he has sacrificed all his ideals along the way, and his, according to the author, is a ruined life.

As background for Dan Meredith's career, Huston carefully reports on the local political scene, the machine control, the neatly stage-managed rallies and campaigns, the

---

[11] The semi-idealized sketches of Stoney Pike in Lester Cohen's *Coming Home* (1945) and Mike Slattery in John O'Hara's *Ten North Frederick* (1955) serve as still other illustrations.

mud-slinging among the candidates, the manipulating of convention delegates, the financing of political operations by undercover methods—in fact, the entire series of devious practices by which a tight little oligarchy is maintained in power.

A Mississippi senator, Gus Roberts, in many respects follows the Meredith model in Edward Kimbrough's *From Hell to Breakfast* (1941). Roberts progressed from governor to senator by virtue of the nicely organized machine behind him, by his skillful if empty ("You still gotta spill the baloney") oratory, and by his hold upon the common people. Playing upon the prejudices of the latter—delivering impassioned speeches for prohibition, against the teaching of the principle of evolution, cursing the Pope and Zionism, the vested interests and Communist plots, and promising twenty-cent cotton—he firmly entrenched himself. His state was changing to a degree, however, and his anti-Red, anti-nigger "line" was losing its appeal. His opposition, mostly in the form of the intelligent and socially-minded young lawyer Jerry Clinton, grew stronger, too, and at the end of the book Gus Roberts' reign is all but over. He had prostrated his genuine liking for the people, says Kimbrough, before his lust for power.

The modern political novelists, like their predecessors, then, are bent upon exposure, exposure of the corruption in federal, state, county, and city government, revealing that the bosses, the lobbyists, the corporation executives, and the officeholders themselves pursue a cynical course. The few idealists in view are usually thwarted, the "people" remain in the background either hoodwinked or indolent, and reform, if it appears, is not lasting. Although bossism has lessened, the political power of racketeering rings has been checked, and the influence-peddlers have occasionally been routed out of Washington, yet no steady movement of reform can be observed. The novelists themselves do not emerge with solutions, other than repeating their predecessors—"better" men must "go in for" politics, the worship of mammon must cease, the sleeping people must awaken and substitute idealism for the shaking of the plum tree, and action for a lazy acceptance of the *status quo.*

Once again the aesthetic strong point of the writers seems to be their accurate rendition of local color. The plotting in the corner saloon, the operations of the lobbyist at a Washington ball, the debates of a Congressional committee, the campaigns in the farm country—of these the reader enjoys a very precise view. Fletcher Knebel and Charles Bailey, in their best-selling *Convention* (1964), briskly unfold the activities of what H. L. Mencken insisted was the most entertaining of circuses, a national political convention. Less briskly but very graphically, Eugene Burdick and Harvey Wheeler, in *Fail-Safe* (1962), recount the operational procedures of the country's higher echelon, the political-military group inevitably linked in these years of continued "cold war." The war room at Omaha, the bomb shelter under the White House, and the conference room at the Pentagon assume a chilling reality.

The presence of knowledgeable detail does not automatically turn a book into an artistic triumph, however, and, regrettably, most of the post-World War I political novels cannot stand as superior examples of the form. The books seldom escape from the documentary category; as such they may photograph politics accurately but scarcely rise above the level of factual studies. Their themes receive such uncomplicated expositions, the problems of their characters such undramatized ("Only an interplay between private conscience and public standard redeems fiction set in public life")[12] treatment, their mechanics such scant attention, that the term "mere documentary" really does apply.

The current crop of political novels—books like *Convention* and *Fail-Safe*, Peter Scaevola's *'68* (1964), and Henry J. Taylor's *The Big Man* (1964)—illustrate the point. The authors are well acquainted with the political environment, it is true. They can speak with authority about campaigns and conventions and can populate their books with a vast array of political types: national committeemen, ghost writers, money raisers, statisticians, press agents, campaign managers, "issues" men and columnists. They introduce the lure of the "topical," too, referring to presidential seizures of steel mills, using Taft-like senators as foils for their power-driven protagonists, discussing the convention credentials of the two delegations from Mississippi, and stressing the importance of the "wholesome" TV image for the political candidates.

Even so, their versions of contemporary politics suffer—occasionally from naïveté, more often from shallowness. The reader is uncomfortably startled when, in Taylor's *The Big Man*, the experienced politician Walter Karnes chooses to break a nominating convention deadlock by the introduc-

---

[12] Edwin M. Yoder, Jr., review of James Hulbert's *Noon on the Third Day* (1962), *Saturday Review*, Vol. 45 (September 8, 1962), 50.

tion of a totally unknown candidate, lawyer Frank Killory, or when Killory, well along in his campaign, suddenly realizes that he must have a "home" state as a base. The reader is distressed when he witnesses the absence of speculative thinking about political concepts, when he observes the black-or-white character divisions, when he senses the author's special pleading and emotion-filled tones. He would prefer introspection to explanation, would like a less superficial view of character (Governor Jim Bob Cole of Kentucky is a vivid caricature, *but* a caricature), would appreciate a less hostile perspective.

The political novelist may be permitted his angry tone, of course, yet one is troubled when his emotions overwhelm his judgment.[13] However willing one is to agree with the thesis of Peter Scaevola in '68 that the far right wing in American politics which sees a Communist under every bush is a dangerously irrational movement, he can but object to the obvious exaggerations of the Scaevola account of anti-Semitism smears, Freedom Legions, and "stamp out treason, vote for Reason" rallies.

The novelists exhibit some glaring weaknesses of technique as well. *The Big Man,* though theoretically concentrating on the campaigns of Frank Killory, shifts hither and yon, frequently neglecting Killory for superfluous sketches of this or that minor character. The Scaevola novel is also a jumble of scenes, despite having a clearly defined channel of communication in its first person narrator Jim van der

[13] As Willard Thorp reminds us, if the writer "is too passionate about the issues he is concerned with, his novel may become more a tract for the times than a work of fiction." Thorp, *op. cit.,* 138–39.

Haag. The dreams, the flashbacks, and the time and place leaps constantly blur the focus. Burdick and Wheeler, in *Fail-Safe*, interrupt their narrative flow to lecture the reader on the operations of a SAC base or to insert a chapter on a character's background. It is amazing how engrossing the novel still remains. The same may be said of *Convention*, which also has a hit-or-miss structure, marred by the authors' "asides" and by the tacked-on love affair between Kay Orcutt and Archie DuPage, yet holds the reader all the way to its resounding climax.

The styles of the novels impress one no more than the structural designs. Taylor's incredible dialogue and sentimental passages, Scaevola's chop-chop-chop sentences, Burdick and Wheeler's stiff expository sequences compare unfavorably with the efforts of so inadequate a stylist as David Graham Phillips. *Convention* shows no particular improvement. It indulges in stilted character vignettes ("It was Carl Fleischer, the Roberts campaign manager, a man whose smoked glasses, shiny gray summer suits, and pocket-size leather pill case were familiar trade-marks in Republican politics") and tiresome slanginess ("But what a guy! Manchester was made for the White House"), and dutifully trots out rather tired figures of speech ("like billows of steam in a Turkish bath") at intervals.

One must conclude that many of the recent political fictions simply "boil the pot." Fortunately, however, a few "superior examples" do exist, and we shall hope to redress the balance to some degree with a subsequent discussion of these.

126

CHAPTER VIII

The Doctrinal Barrage (1920-1964)

THE group of "attackers" whose works we have just been reviewing do not account for all the contemporary discussion, in fiction, of political affairs. Many novelists were not laying down barrages directed against malfunctioning political machinery and the malevolent operators of it, but were intent upon criticizing certain political ideologies which they regarded as suspect. A whole battery of books, ranging from Sinclair Lewis' *It Can't Happen Here* (1935) to John Dos Passos' *Chosen Country* (1951) discuss political loyalties and ideological identifications, endeavoring to dramatize these abstractions and propagandize for or against them. Fascism, Marxism, liberalism, conservatism—a host of "isms" serve the authors' turn in their fight for social and political change.

It must be said at the outset that these doctrinal discussions seldom fully measure up to their European models. Chester Eisinger's statement about the influence of such examples as Silone, Malraux, and Orwell should be borne in mind:

It is the liberal or the leftist writer abroad who made in fiction the enduring answer to totalitarianism. Ignazio Silone, for instance, is a heroic figure in his insistence on the kind of political life that will keep the writer free and in his enduring posture of sturdy dissent. He has brought his ideas, living and dramatic, into his fiction in a way that no American novelist has been able to do; no American has utilized the body of liberal democratic principles the way Silone has utilized his blend of social, Christian ideas. These principles have rarely been fused in America into the kind of political novel that Irving Howe defines: one in which representations of human experience and feeling and relationships are brought together with an idea of society which penetrates the lives and consciousness of the characters and makes them fully alive to political ideas and loyalties.[1]

There are isolated instances, nonetheless, of American novels which satisfy the Howe definition, and even those which do not altogether realize their opportunities succeed in engendering reader interest.

In the 1930's, Fascism abroad and the possibility of dictatorship at home aroused many a writer, Lewis' *It Can't Happen Here*, for example, serving as one response. Having in mind the Huey Longs, Father Coughlins, and Gerald L. K. Smiths, who, he felt, exhibited Hitler-like tendencies, Lewis launched a ferocious tirade, suggesting that it might very well "happen here" just as it already had in Germany.

According to the Lewis account, Senator Buzz Windrip, owing to the hysterical climate prevailing in America, gets himself nominated and elected President and quickly becomes a dictator. The country, infested with figures like the blandly militaristic General Edgeways, the stupid DAR leader Mrs. Ada Gimmitch, the bigoted Dewey Haik, proves

[1] Chester E. Eisinger, *Fiction of the Forties*, 98.

128

ripe for a dictatorship and is easily taken in by Buzz the demagogue. Only one plank in Buzz's vague platform registers with the voters, the seeming promise that each man would soon have five thousand dollars. The voters, all selfish as well as imperceptive, happily elect him, not bothered by the Minute Men who surround him, nor by the glib emptiness of his oratory. An awakening comes to some individuals quite quickly, however, as they watch Windrip control legislation, allow only one political party, and set off a wave of terrorism. The regime becomes ever more autocratic and bloody, people being shot or dispatched to concentration camps, suspicious books burned, education subverted, and purges introduced. The rationalizing supporters of the Windrip method, such as Philip Jessup, insist that one can forgive the means if the end is sound (in this case it obviously is not), but others deny such a Machiavellian theory.

Among these others is Philip's father, Doremus Jessup, a "liberal" editor. Together with a handful of rebellious souls, Doremus has distrusted Windrip from the outset. This opposition force goes underground in order to combat the Windrip regime (a Communist group operates separately; Jessup does not approve of their methods) and does inflict some damage on the rulers. The governmental leaders also harm their own cause by an intramural fight for power. Yet the dictatorship remains in the saddle at the book's end.

Lewis does hold out a hope that the liberals may eventually effect a change. A Doremus Jessup never dies, he declares; the liberal—the free, inquiring, critical spirit—will in the long run preserve some of the arts of civilization. In view of the unrelieved gloom of the picture he has previously painted, however, this hope seems too much like late-in-the-day wishful thinking.

Although critics at the time of the book's publication praised it as a major political act,[2] the examination of Fascism in *It Can't Happen Here* really does not progress beyond the superficial. An arresting tour de force, yes, and fascinating in its detailed imaginative reconstruction of how the country's political structure would be reorganized under a dictatorship, yet the novel is vitiated by Lewis' uncertain grasp of the problems raised by a fascistic regime ("off with their heads" is only *one* dictatorial response) and by his failure to insert an adequate antidote. He wishes us to accept, as an antidote, the liberal position of Doremus Jessup, and we should like to do so, were we perfectly sure what position Jessup had assumed. If his vague middle-of-the-road stance contents the author, it does not satisfy the reader. The work thus lacks intellectual coherence and persuasiveness.

Moreover, as an artistic effort, it suffers in several respects. Failing to make adroit use of its fantasy form, the book does not achieve the imaginative consistency of a *Brave New World* or the nightmare vision of *1984*. It is not quite safe to operate on the principle that "anything goes" in a fantasy—the reader simply refuses to accept scenes such as the Navy CPO's battle with the Minute Men or Mary Greenhill's diving her plane on that of Effingham Swan—nor can a writer maintain a nightmare vision if he makes his villain wildly comic and if he even chuckles at his hero.

So wrapped up in publicizing the evils of Fascism is Lewis in *It Can't Happen Here* that he neglects to show adequate

[2] Mark Schorer, *Sinclair Lewis*, 609.

concern over the aesthetics of the novel. Adopting, as so often before, an excessively satiric and strident tone, he wearies the reader with his extravagances, with the elaborate satire at the expense of Bishop Paul Peter Prang, the savage denunciation of the stupid foreign press, the nasty potshots at "real" people like Senator Theodore Bilbo and Upton Sinclair.

Forgetting the warning that "characters in the political novel are always in danger of becoming walking ideas,"[3] he creates people who "represent" things rather than people who are many-sided and alive. One is willing to permit him, as a fantasist, to introduce caricatures and exaggerated portraits, and thus one will not quibble too much about the Honorable J. S. Reek, Mr. Cowlick (though regretting Lewis' reliance on the age-old device of supposedly funny proper names), or loutish Shad Ledue, but he does wish the Jessup family and their friends carried more conviction, as also the Communist, Karl Pascal, a mouthpiece rather than a man.

Lewis seems to function on a rather haphazard structural theory, too (dipping back and forth between Windrip and the national scene, Jessup and the local scene), and he is guilty of other technical flaws. Too often he employs parallelism and cataloguing ("most of the mortgaged farmers . . . most of the white-collar workers . . . most of the people on relief rolls . . . most of the suburbanites"), or piles up details to an excessive degree (we learn far more than we want, or need, to know about the Jessup background, family, house). Many sequences are overwritten, both the melo-

[3] John McCormick, *Catastrophe and Imagination*, 234.

dramatic action bits like the arrests and inquisitions and also the slangy dialogue (Lewis' gift for mimicry is, in my opinion, much overrated), and the figurative language is, conversely, drab. We must heartily second Lewis' own comment: "It isn't a very good book."[4]

Many of the writers who joined Lewis in attacking the "leader cult" chose to center their fictions on an actual figure, the "Louisiana Kingfish," Huey Long. A dictator in the fascist pattern, the majority agree, and one who came close to making an affirmation out of Lewis' "It can't happen here."

Long, a poor white, meagerly educated and perpetually embittered, was motivated by an unbridled ambition and a desire for power which his sometimes noble-sounding platform could not mask.[5] His share-the-wealth program, for example, was really a deliberate attempt to exploit the ignorance, prejudices, and economic misery of the rural population of Louisiana. His scheme of education and public works was financed by heavy taxation of corporations, utilities, and private wealth. His seemingly socialized economy resulted in enormous profits for his underlings and himself. In other words, said many at the time of his "reign," he used the institutions of democracy to eradicate democracy from the state of Louisiana.

In the 1940's four novels about this troublesome political figure appeared: Hamilton Basso's *Sun In Capricorn* (1942), John Dos Passos' *Number One* (1943), Adria Locke Langley's *A Lion Is In the Streets* (1945), and Robert Penn

---

[4] Quoted in Schorer, *op. cit.*, 611.

[5] According to Harold Gosnell, "There is little indication that Long had any elaborate or well-thought-out social program." Harold F. Gosnell, *Grass Roots Politics*, 113.

Warren's *All the King's Men* (1946). All the books report the same general outline of his life—the upward course of the "barefoot boy with cheek." In writing of his quick rise from a peddling job in the barren Bible belt of upstate Louisiana to a place in the United States Senate, the novelists emphasize both his "brassy idiom, hammy histrionics and cotton patch demagoguery"[6] and also the totalitarian trimmings of his program. With the exception of Warren, they see him as only in small measure a reformer, much more thoroughly a cynical politician, and therefore they waste little sympathy upon him.

To Hamilton Basso, Long was Gilgo Slade, a "peckerwood" lawyer, who secured office by a liberal distribution of cornmeal to his constituents and by charming them with a hillbilly band and with corn pone and pot-liquor contests. Once in office, he carefully maintained his "one-of-the-boys" approach, meeting the Spanish ambassador in a pair of tan shorts and a tan undershirt, and surrounding himself with circus atmosphere calculated to catch the fancy of his "poor white" following. In his personal entourage were included the gunman Hard-Jaws and his secretary, Fritz Cowan, whose job it was to ferret out ugly facts in the lives of Gilgo's enemies.

His standard political tactic was the ranting and roaring speech, with equal emphasis on Biblical quotations and the "I'm a one-suit man like you" refrain. Basso shows the man's tremendous egoism, ambition, energy, cleverness, and ability to lead, but he also shows that Gilgo did not really care about the "peepul," whom he frankly regarded as so many

6 Leo Gurko, *The Angry Decade*, 182.

"boobs," and that he forged ahead by dishonest means, lying, slandering, buying votes. At the end of the novel two supporters of Slade discuss him: the greatest man since Jesus Christ, says one; a smart bastard, says the other. It is easy to discern with whom Basso would agree.

To John Dos Passos, Huey Long, alias Chuck Crawford, appears, in a similar light. He shares with Gilgo Slade the energy, ambition, egotism, champion-of-the-people role, and utter unscrupulousness. If sometimes the latter characteristic could be explained away on the grounds of just customary "political practice"—*i.e.*, securing the governor's reluctant endorsement of his senatorial candidacy by some wirepulling, or slandering his "enemy-of-the-people" opponent Fatty Galbraith—at other times it could not. The shady business deals, by means of which he grows very prosperous, cannot be condoned on any grounds, nor can his sacrifice of his devoted supporter, Tyler Spotswood, when his empire threatens to topple about him. Chuck Crawford, bodyguard-surrounded, power-mad, far more closely resembles a fascist dictator than he does the Lincoln with whom he likes to be compared.

Both Basso and Dos Passos catch interesting facets of their central character, his superb evangelism and common touch as well as his unbridled ambition and underhanded strategy, yet neither author moves him far away from the dictator stereotype. Lesser characters—such as Dos Passos' Tyler Spotswood, undergoing a severe moral conflict with regard to his leader, Crawford—achieve more actuality.

Adria Langley calls Huey Long Hank Martin and likens him to the big lion, king of the jungle. Hank becomes "king" by cleverness and chicanery. Knowing how to handle the common people, he receives almost fanatical support from them, yet he does not really care at all about them as individuals; they are just voters. His real goal is not even the vague paternalism that his program suggests, but simply power for himself. He progresses by using gangster-type methods, by bribery, by "arrangements" with gamblers, by dredging up a "grandpappy" law which makes many illiterates eligible to vote, and by his "kindling power" among the masses. Once in the gubernatorial chair, he amasses substantial profits for himself, employing the "kickback" system and other "nictitating" means, and he turns the office into a dictatorship.

At the end of the novel author Langley says—with very little conviction—that Hank Martin could have been great. He was, to use his own words, "purely gulled." *But* he was gulled by flaws in his own character, ignorance, self-centeredness, a power mania,[7] and a forgetfulness of the people whom he has supposedly championed.

Mrs. Langley chooses to tell her story of the "big lion" through the eyes of his wife Verity, an unfortunate choice of point of view since it establishes sentimentality as the dominant mood and overemphasizes the "lover-boy" side of Hank's character. The presence of some baffling dialect and of highly overdrawn characters (e.g., Gerald L. K. Smith

[7] Again and yet again the political novel resolves itself into a discussion of power. One is reminded of the definition of a politician offered by a writer for the *Times Literary Supplement:* ". . . a politician, however good-willed, must be a person who wants to command and manipulate the machinery of power, at best a person who thinks he knows better than others how their lives should be run." "Politics or Commitment?" *Times Literary Supplement* (September 1, 1961), 580. Some of the novels in C. P. Snow's Lewis Eliot series neatly support this definition.

as Saber Milady) also contributes to the general ineffectiveness of the work. Mrs. Langley's attitude toward language and point of view and the tactics of fictional craft tends toward the utilitarian.

A much finer book, and the best of the four—the thoroughly professional Dos Passos and the only less thoroughly professional Basso do not distinguish themselves in their Huey Long novels—is that by Robert Penn Warren, whose portrait shows more complexity and more sympathy. The Willie Stark of *All the King's Men* had, Warren feels, a worthwhile political program and an impressive quality, or "greatness," about him.

> Perhaps he spilled it on the ground the way you spill a liquid when the bottle breaks. Perhaps he piled up his greatness and burnt it in one great blaze in the dark like a bonfire. . . . Perhaps he could not tell his greatness from ungreatness and so mixed them together that what was adulterated was lost. But he had it.

Warren suggests—and the others roughly agree—that Huey Long had a chance to become a great Democrat but was turned aside by excessive ambition and self-centeredness into what came close to being Fascism.[8]

If the threat of Fascism preoccupied many a modern political novelist, it did not engage the attention of all. Some were caught up in still other "isms," racialism, bureaucratism, socialism, Communism, liberalism, conservatism—a diversified spectrum. One can even find attacks on capitalism, at least in the depression thirties when the Marxist

[8] *All the King's Men* will be treated in detail in the next chapter.

novel enjoyed a great vogue. Lewis Browne's *Oh, Say, Can You See?* (1937), for example, reports on the reactions of a Russian ichthyologist and Communist, who can "see" some virtues but also many weaknesses in the American capitalistic system. Most of the books on this topic, however, can more accurately be labeled economic rather than political novels, and thus they remain outside the realm of my discussion.[9]

The polar extreme of capitalism, Marxism, was at the same time a target in the 1930's and has become an increasingly popular subject in the decades which have followed. John Dos Passos' *Adventures of a Young Man* (1938) may be singled out as among the more subtle treatments of this ideology. Dos Passos, rather than indulging in an out-and-out denunciation, puts before the reader both the strengths and weaknesses of the dogma, offering in his protagonist, Glenn Spotswood, an idealistic individual, who has been guided by worthy if not altogether farseeing motives in embracing Communism, and who remains loyal until he is finally convinced of the shortcomings of the Party.

It is enlightening to read the book at the present time, to see how genuine liberals like Glenn Spotswood could have become affiliated with the Communist movement. One must bear in mind the Party's role in the 1930's as champion of the underdog, as backer of the exploited pecan shellers in Texas or the miners in Pennsylvania.

Glenn Spotswood is attracted to such endeavors, and it takes him some time to realize that the Marxist leaders are opportunistically using the shellers and the miners to obtain

[9] Such fiction is very adequately discussed in Walter Rideout's *The Radical Novel in the United States, 1900–1954.*

publicity for themselves, to strengthen the Party's control, to raise a huge political *brouhaha* in order to secure for themselves a new crop of martyrs—all the while not caring about the workers as individuals at all. Glenn also learns—eventually—that Marxism, since the death of Lenin, has grown less "idealistic," that, for example, Marxists are participating in the Spanish Civil War for selfish reasons rather than for the cause of liberty in the abstract. Disillusioned, he shakes off the Party line, and, for his pains, is excommunicated and subsequently murdered. Dos Passos thus firmly rejects Marxism, though only after a reasonably deliberate weighing of the merits and demerits of its tenets and practice.

Dissatisfied with both Fascism and Communism, Dos Passos turns for solace, in *The Grand Design* (1949),[10] to "democratic" bureaucracy, as embodied in the New Deal. Its aim, a more equable society, pleases him, of course, yet he feels called upon to question the achievements of the "movement" and the genuineness of its "liberalism." The New Deal personnel, men of relatively low caliber for the most part, steer the nation uncertainly, some of them succumbing to influence-peddlers, some of them being fooled by left-wingers who merely feign a belief in democratic processes.

Dos Passos also implies that Mr. Big (F.D.R.) grows more autocratic as World War II approaches, and that New Deal principles, such as a decent wage level, collective bargaining, and the like, tend to be forgotten by all but a few.

[10] The last volume in his trilogy *District of Columbia*, preceded by the aforementioned *Adventures of a Young Man* and *Number One*. The trilogy, Chester Eisinger says, offers three varieties of political experience, first, a rejection of Communism, second, of native Fascism, third, of centralized bureaucracy. Eisinger, *op. cit.*, 121.

Concluding that the Good American is victimized by the forces of corruption and compromise in his society, Dos Passos demands recognition of the falsity of purely material standards, encourages a return to Jeffersonian agrarianism and individualism, and stresses the importance of a truly liberal attitude.[11]

Dos Passos' political fiction—most notably the *District of Columbia* trilogy—contains many acute social insights and displays his immense narrative gift and ability to create realistic characters, particularly the "heroes," Glenn Spotswood, Tyler Spotswood, Millard Carroll, all embroiled in valid plights. The various segments of society constructed around them come to life as well, and the author's flatly ironic style—functioning except in the superfluous prose poem interludes—seems appropriate. If not so remarkable an achievement as the earlier Dos Passos trilogy, *USA*, *District of Columbia* adds up to a distinct accomplishment, by a man more touched than most by political concern, and more skilled than most in dramatizing that concern.

For a still more convincing statement of the interplay of human experience and political idea, however, we turn to Lionel Trilling's *The Middle of the Journey* (1947), a volume given over to a searching and stimulating discussion of the "liberal" political position. Taking the New Deal decade and the years immediately following as his province, Trilling enumerates the several approaches to liberalism made

---

11 In the words of Willard Thorp, "America is still his 'chosen country' but because it has been betrayed again and again by the politicians, the money-makers, the Communists and the gullible liberals, the only comfort an honest man can find is to go back to the roots, to find 'the ground we stand on.'" Thorp, *op. cit.*, 138.

by a characteristic group of troubled intellectuals, all, in theory, wanting to improve the lot of those living in the "confused thirties," but all offering different—and conflicting—ways to effect improvement.

At one extreme one finds Kermit Simpson, the politically idealistic owner of *The New Era*, a "rather sad" because muddled-in-its-thinking liberal monthly. Both the magazine and its owner represent a simple and gentle liberal and humanitarian faith, but, to quote Simpson's friend John Laskell, both are "chuckleheaded" and prove inconsequential in their propagandizing. Although a conscientious do-gooder, Simpson fails, despite his wealth and kind intentions, because he is bemused by the causes which he espouses and by the people whom he endorses. For example, Simpson will unquestioningly employ Gifford Maxim as a writer for his magazine, not perceiving that Maxim has become a thoroughgoing reactionary and thus one hardly equipped to support *The New Era*'s liberal position. Again, when, toward the end of the book, the principals are engaged in a most acrimonious and splintering discussion, in which we see friendship disintegrating in the face of sharply differing political opinions, Simpson remains perfectly at ease, because "to Kermit a difference of opinion was a difference of opinion and showed that liberalism still flourished."

At the other extreme from "innocent" Kermit Simpson stands the cynical ex-Marxist Gifford Maxim. The latter had, some years before the book opens, carried "liberalism" to the ultimate in joining the Communist Party. Maxim had functioned as a thorough revolutionary, believing in the "bloody and apocalyptic and moral future," as a professional, believing that results rather than the means (which might be brutal) mattered. Although partly motivated by concern for the suffering men of the world, he was also motivated, along with his fellow Communists, by the selfish desire for power. But at the time of the book's commencement, he has renounced his allegiance and in fact slanders the "cause for which he had fought so long." Reversing himself completely, he now pleads for the maintenance of the *status quo* ("I am for the leaders"), and for a reliance upon religious faith.

His change, and the man himself, are regarded with suspicion by John Laskell (the book's protagonist, and, one feels, the author's spokesman). Laskell bases his distrust on two grounds, first, on the belief that, however good the reasons that make a man desert his cause, he will always be unpleasant to see, his moral equilibrium unable to restore itself. Maxim is monomaniacally obsessed with the fear that the Party is determined to have him rubbed out (he must take the last seat in the last car on the train), and he is almost equally obsessed with spreading "foul and melodramatic" stories about the Party. These signs of instability not only greatly bother Laskell, but leave him quite perturbed. Laskell's distrust stems, secondly, from his conviction that Maxim is insincere as well as unbalanced. The latter has too cynically and too glibly adopted his conservative position. Explaining his new stand with the flat statement, "I am going to secure my safety," he demonstrates a selfishness sharply contrasting with his former idealistic aim of improving the welfare of the masses. Moreover, though he pretends to a religious faith, quoting Saint Paul and tossing words like

141

"mercy" and "mysteries" and the "unseen" around, these
are words, Laskell reflects, which he had used, for quite different purposes, when unfolding the Marxist line, and they
seem to have no real meaning for him. Laskell thus feels that
Maxim's present view is both not genuine and—more repre-
hensible still—not at all liberal. If Maxim proclaims that we
are all members one of another, yet he has lost his sense of
community with men in their suffering (his is a "practiced
solicitude") and found it only in their cruelty—a negative approach. Furthermore, he puts his faith, now, in the stand-
patters and is indeed an apostate. Laskell regrets that a "mind
so fine" has become so "distorted."

Other friends of Laskell's, Nancy and Arthur Croom, belong, as had Maxim, to the "concerned" intelligentsia, worried about the "pain of the time" in which they live, and
seeking a proper way to cope with it. But in Laskell's opinion
they are confused people and their "way" inadequate. Arthur Croom represents the man of action, the administrator,
intelligent and sympathetic, yet one who insists a little too
strongly on "reality," on "doing," and thus ignores the value
of dreams and visionary ideas. Laskell labels him the man of
the "*near* future," one whose intelligence and character
would permit him to make a go of things for a while, but only
for a while, for he lacks the comprehensive view and too
often exhibits shortsightedness.

His wife also thinks in terms of the immediate—what she
calls the "real"—and has an even more confined view. She
"would have liked to hurry . . . the reality of the better
future into being." The key word in this phrase is "hurry."
Nancy Croom, possessing the reformer mentality, can see

only one side of an issue, will brook no opposition, and must "hurry" to her goal. She has already assisted the Communists (having received letters for Maxim, when he was a Party member), ignoring the fact that their any-means-to-the-end position does not harmonize with her basic ethical view, and at present she is flirting with the idea of joining the Party, thereby taking action rather than being content with "liberal shilly-shallying talk." The country is so threatened by enemies, she says, that it cannot afford liberal notions of justice, and thus might utilize, it is implied, the ruthless Party methods.

One-track-minded as she is, Nancy makes herself see only the good in Communism, overlooking its failure to make a place for individual responsibility and the need for mercy. Laskell admires her ardor and idealism, her firm desire to "preach the law for the masses," but he cannot accept her too dogmatic, often inconsistent, often misguided, approach.

Laskell himself would assume a more temperate, though not necessarily passive, position. Objecting to the radicals (Communists *or* ex-Communists) as too extreme, he would not, on the other hand, accept the Croom type of "fellow-travelling" liberal, whose view is, in its way, just as narrow. Concerned like the others (save Maxim) with making the world better, yet he appraises the present more thoughtfully and entertains somewhat less sanguine hopes for the future, though no less desire to work toward a happier one. A liberal in the best sense, as he sees it, is one who keeps his mind open to new ideas, who maintains humanitarian sympathies, but who always aims for the sensible position, for the balanced perspective. If ready to accept the Marxist goal of aiding suffering and exploited men, he is not ready to accept its method, a reliance upon sheer power, nor its blind conformity to the commissars.

Laskell would, in every instance, employ to the best of his ability the "humanistic, critical intelligence" in endeavoring to cope with the world. This means acting "in modulation"—*but* acting. It is not acquiesence, not passivity, but it *is* moderation. Thus, as John Laskell reaches "the middle of the journey," he assumes a "middle of the road" stance, one that may, unhappily, cause alienation from his friends, but one that represents the most tenable kind of liberalism, Laskell and author Trilling agree.

In and around this ideological discussion, which serves as the core of the book, Trilling weaves various speculations about the large subjects of death and love, relating these to his political topic by virtue of the belief that undergirds his remarks in every instance, the need for human beings to adopt a responsible attitude.

The death motif is established early in the novel, in the sequence dealing with Laskell's serious illness and recovery and his reactions to his experience. Trilling stresses the fact that Laskell, during his convalescence, is "half in love with easeful death," enjoying a "white, endless peace" and yearning for its perpetuation. From this unhealthy preoccupation he eventually recovers, aided principally by his affair with Emily Caldwell, an association which removes "the carping remnants of his illness." To be sure, he remains "in love with death a little," as Emily puts it, and why should he not? One must accept the omnipresence of death, as she, having a daughter with a weak heart, very well knows. Laskell endorses this point of view; Nancy Croom, on the other hand, will not. She refuses to listen to talk of his recent illness, and attempts to shut out the fact of death, even when directly confronted with it, as in the case of the tragedy befalling Susan Caldwell. But her ostrich-like attitude must be rejected, so Trilling implies. The sane view, exemplified in Emily Caldwell, agonized at the loss of her daughter yet regaining her balance and going on, should prevail.

The love motif appears early, too—in the first scene of the novel, when Laskell, contentedly anticipating a visit with his friends the Crooms, then momentarily shaken by their nonappearance on the station platform, feels that all will soon be put to rights by their company, by the "peace of affection." The Crooms do "take him in" and "cherish" him, but almost immediately their relationship becomes strained, tension resulting from their political differences, a tension that will not subside. During the remainder of the novel the "abysses of feeling" continue to open, causing this most firm friendship to rest at last on a very shaky foundation. Such is also the case with the Laskell-Maxim relationship, even the Laskell-Simpson one. None of them could make a permanent "connection."

Other "connections" outlined in the novel prove equally tenuous: Laskell's nurse Paine, his very good friend while he is sick, is glad to leave him when he is restored to health; Mrs. Folger, his friendly landlady in the country, is not sorry to see him go—"he was out of connection, merely a summer boarder ready to leave"; the love affair between Emily Caldwell and Laskell, pleasant and helpful though it may be, is nonetheless inevitably a transient one. The bonds of love, affection, and companionability may be temporary or easily forestalled. In the light of this hard fact of life, the sane view must again be adopted. One should be prepared for the unpredictability of love, as for the omnipresence of death, understanding the moment-to-moment dangers of the difficult business of living, recognizing that the mature human being is involved in "tragic responsibility."

The chief characters in *The Middle of the Journey* are equated, as we have seen, with intellectual positions: Simpson the gullible liberal, Maxim the selfish reactionary, Nancy and Arthur Croom the headlong devotees of liberal shibboleths, Laskell the temperate liberal. At the same time they are made to seem believable individuals rather than simply "walking ideas."

Kermit Simpson, for example, relieves his bland optimism by a "queer grace" and seems very human as he proudly demonstrates the gadgets in his elegant trailer. The complexity of Nancy Croom is suggested by the reader's mixed feelings about her. Attracted by her grace as a wife and mother and by her charm and "shining affirmations," he is, contrarily, put off by her dogmatism and her manifold confusions. She exasperates one in her failure to see behind Emily Caldwell's pretensions to the genuine person beneath and, conversely, to see behind her admiring concept of Duck Caldwell as the native American proletarian to the reality of Duck, an evil and empty-minded person. Her inconsistencies —accepting the absolutism of Stalinism but finding the absolutism of Christianity madness, wishing to destroy tradition yet insisting on an old-fashioned picnic—irritate one

146

also, but her very flaws contribute, of course, to the actuality of her portrait.

Trilling's sympathetic, if low-toned protagonist, John Laskell, is particularly well drawn and convincingly embodies the "rounded" view that his creator endorses. Highly perceptive, he appraises his associates correctly, the Caldwells, the Crooms, Maxim, and the others. Maxim's essay on "Billy Budd," for instance, about the tragedy of spirit and law in a world of necessity, Laskell reads correctly as an impassioned plea for the *status quo*, the accepted thing, the rule of force. The Crooms, in contrast, biased by their preconceptions, do not properly evaluate the essay. Most important, Laskell appraises himself correctly, too, questioning his possible loss of "moral ambition" as he approaches the "middle of the journey," sensing his own irresponsibility in his earlier relationship with Elizabeth Fuess, appreciating the harm in his entanglement with the Caldwell family. Laskell comes through to the reader as a humane, humorous, clear-sighted, morally concerned man and thus a thoroughly likable (even if faintly priggish) individual and a thoroughly acceptable representative of the "mediate" view.

Trilling has good luck with his minor characters also, as in his sketch of the craggy Miss Paine, or the boorish Duck Caldwell, summed up in the "lurch and swagger" of his walk. Others in the gallery, the minister Mr. Gurney, about whom everything was all too clear, Miss Debry, the stupid small-town belle type with the "foolish little social mind," Mr. Folger, the "interesting bore," and the local aristocrat Miss Walker, "only a little package of an elderly maiden lady, dowdy and graceless," clearly pass muster, too. Trilling avoids, both with his principals and those in secondary roles, one of the pitfalls of the "idea novel," the talker type who simply "stands for" something and has no individuality.

Among the technical virtues of *The Middle of the Journey*, one would list its precise pattern. The book is neatly organized around the political dialectic, the Crooms and Simpson perhaps representing thesis, Maxim, antithesis, and Laskell, synthesis.[12] Trilling also balances his structure by deftly intermingling action and conversation, drama and "good talk." As the story develops, he unobtrusively inserts expository flashbacks, and he constantly steps up the pace of the novel by increasing the tension in the political discussions (*q.v.*, the scene in which Nancy Croom calls Gifford Maxim by his last name and he replies in kind), moving to an exciting climax with the death of Susan Caldwell. A logical denouement follows, the plan for separation ("he was utterly weary of his friends"), a final fruitless debate, and then the various departures, the "connections" severed.

Trilling employs a lucid and easy, yet clever and sophisticated style in the novel, one which seems well adapted, too, to the focal character, John Laskell, whose point of view we follow throughout. The sentences proceed quietly and are often deliberately underplayed: "It was nice and Laskell said so," "It could be thought of that way, and Laskell decided that that was the way he would think of it." The figures of speech are extracted from the everyday world, e.g., "each day was like a fresh sheet on his bed." On the other hand, esoteric allusions sprinkle the pages, and donnish words like "sequester" appear. Trilling even introduces

12 Eisinger, *op. cit.*, 143.

rhetorical tricks ("firm excitement or excited firmness") and sets up Jamesian echoes in his play with adverbs (Emily's bowl "so thoroughly not good"). One may safely say that the style is marked by a deceptive simplicity, the laconic understatement and crystal clarity at first glance concealing Trilling's precision. His succinct description of Gifford Maxim as "a man in whom one could almost hear the dim, slow sound of disintegration," his deliberately formal summation of a gingerly encounter—"It was not hostility, but a very stiff meeting of wills in full panoply" and his concise observations ("It was one of those antagonisms that give great moral satisfaction to both parties") reflect an art that conceals art, and one deserving of praise.

As he canvasses his subject, Trilling sustains a coolness of tone which is rather unusual for a political novelist. Although treating of very serious matters, and matters about which he feels strongly, he remains for the most part gently ironic. The bite may creep in—Laskell's comment that Nancy talks about morbidity and living in the past as if she thought death politically reactionary—and the book has a melancholy cast, emphasizing as it does the sense of alienation, the failures in "connection,"[13] still, Trilling adheres to his composure and comments ruefully rather than savagely. Because he achieves density in his thoughtful analysis of liberalism and moderation, while at the same time infusing his book with a lifelike spirit, he reaches the standards set by the very best of his contemporaries.

[13] One may cite still other instances of separation, that between Duck Caldwell and the Croom group, for example, or that between Emily Caldwell and Laskell after Susan's death. The city-country gap, too, which Nancy Croom tries unsuccessfully to bridge, provides another illustration.

In the years following World War II, the position of the thinking liberals like Trilling and Dos Passos came to be regarded with suspicion by a large group of Americans, who loosely linking them with Socialist and Communist organizations, chose to accuse all three of a gigantic plot to subvert democratic institutions. Seeking to countermand this "subversion," the group formulated a doctrine which has come to be labeled ultraconservatism or Right Wing-ism—now perhaps Goldwaterism. Rising to prominence during the days of the McCarthy investigations, they attached to themselves from the first the witch-hunting and scapegoat-chasing associations of McCarthyism, and their endless "soft-on-Communism" refrain soon inspired angry reactions from many of their fellow Americans.

One outlet for these reactions proved to be the political novel. Lewis Browne's *See What I Mean* began the trend as early as 1943, and the attack on the "superpatriots" has continued in such novels as Irwin Shaw's *The Troubled Air* (1951), Ruth Chatterton's *The Betrayers* (1953), Tom Wicker's *The Kingpin* (1953), and Peter Scaevola's *'68* (1964). Less concerned with the Conservatives' domestic policy, their fear of governmental centralization, the novelists have preferred to rebuke them for their attitude toward foreign affairs, their "America first" shrillness, excessive suspicions of the State Department, and hysterical susceptibility to demagoguery. The Shaw and Chatterton books may serve as illustrations.

The Troubled Air focuses on the "redbook" incident of the early 1950's, the publication of a book listing the Communists or suspected Communists employed in the radio industry, as entertainers. If "red-listed," individuals were most certainly black-listed and thus fired from their jobs and unable to secure other ones. Many of those whose names appeared, Shaw reminds the reader, had Communist sympathies in the late thirties, a time when it meant for most people a concern for the downtrodden, not a Marxist-led world revolution nor Russian aggression. Should cardholders of that period—usually idealists, if hindsight shows them to be misguided—be branded now? Shaw regrets such a blanket indictment.

He also suggests that the loudest anti-Communists use their anti-Communism to cloak bigotry, a lust for war, approval of dictatorship, in fact, a hatred of all liberalism, progress and freedom of expression. Moreover, he questions their tactics, reminding us that accusation is not evidence, criticism is not heresy, advocacy of change is not treason. Too quick to accuse, overly suspicious and reactionary, and excessively denunciatory, these "defenders of the American way" do far more harm than good. At the same time, Shaw slams the dedicated Communists as well as the narrow-minded inquisitors, pleading for a healthy progressive attitude, which would fall in between these two extremes.

The Betrayers, with an ironic twist, declares that those "defenders of the American way" may well be the real "betrayers" rather than the suspected Communists in government. Miss Chatterton chooses to berate the "insane demagogues" in Congress, who, in the name of patriotism, conduct senatorial investigations which are thoroughly destructive of personal liberties. Senator Floyd Glavis, a thinly veiled portrait of the late Senator McCarthy, is, in the first place, motivated by political strategy and a desire for personal revenge rather than an altruistic concern for the nation's well-being. He then misuses the senatorial investigating power, failing to preserve dignity and justice in the proceedings and resorting to vigilante methods instead.

The victim, Mike Prescott, is suspected simply because he had left-wing political views when in college, is devoted to racial equality, and believes in labor unions and extensive government control of public utilities. But he is labeled as a dangerous "red" and is "railroaded" by Senator Glavis and his committee. The author would prefer that the power of investigation be left primarily in the hands of the FBI, a body which would insure a more equitable treatment.

These ideologically-oriented novels resemble those assailing corruption in making stirring reading and effective emotional propaganda—*q.v.*, the Shaw and Chatterton animus! One does not necessarily find therein complete objectivity, exhaustive expositions of political theory, or constant credibility, but he does discover lucid descriptions of the political environment and of the moral problems arising in such an environment. As he evaluates the "message" contained, his awareness of the complex society in which he lives is usually increased. If he could wish, sometimes, for more subtle analysis and greater literary merit, he has at least the work of Dos Passos and Trilling on which to fall back. *The Middle of the Journey*, in particular, testifies that distinguished use can be made of the novel as a means of advancing—to return to Irving Howe's definition—"an idea of society which penetrates the lives and consciousness of the characters and makes them fully alive to political ideas and loyalties."

☆

CHAPTER IX

Professionals: Warren, O'Connor, and Drury

AMONG the more successful illustrations of the political novel genre in this recent era, one must include three much-discussed books, Robert Penn Warren's *All the King's Men* (1946), Edwin O'Connor's *The Last Hurrah* (1956), and Allen Drury's *Advise and Consent* (1959). All have received the supreme accolade of being placed high on the best-seller list and of being made into moving pictures, and all have received serious critical attention as well.

The first of the three, *All the King's Men*, offers an absorbing account of the career of politician Willie Stark (or Huey Long),[1] while at the same time focusing primarily on the book's narrator, Jack Burden, Stark's secretary. Warren's concern is to summon up an authentic political background and to chart Stark's course against this background—offering these not simply as ends in themselves but as providing Jack Burden with food for thought in evaluating life and endeavoring to find a workable philosophy. The author suc-

---

[1] Warren has always denied making Stark a fictive disguise for Long, but critics and readers alike have gone on making the association, and I choose to join them. One need not press the parallel to the nth degree, yet one may profitably draw the parallel. For a different opinion see Leonard Casper, *Robert Penn Warren, The Dark and Bloody Ground*, xiii. See also Louis D. Rubin, Jr., *The Faraway Country: Writers of the Modern South*, 107ff.

ceeds both in reproducing a credible setting and in developing a thoughtful thesis by means of the characters deployed
against this setting.

As part of his pattern Warren unfolds the progress in
politics of Willie Stark. At first a struggling lawyer from the
shabby red hill country of Louisiana, involved in politics
only to the extent of being county treasurer, Willie is then
introduced into the "big time" by the Harrison forces, practiced politicians in control of the state. This group "uses"
him, however, having selected him as a dummy candidate
who will split the opposition's vote and thus insure Harrison's, not Stark's, winning the governorship. When Willie
realizes he has been played for a sucker, he goes all out to
win the election for Harrison's opponent, and he succeeds.

Important in his "awakening" is his recognition that
idealism has little place in politics and his finding for himself
the tactics which will serve him in good stead thereafter, the
use of the "folksy" approach, of country dialect and barnyard
humor (mixed with quotations from the Scripture), and a
demagogic manipulation of the rural voters—the agrarian
demagogue in the making. It is not long before he has built
up a huge following in the state and has achieved the governorship. In this position he endeavors to do good for the
common people ("your will is my strength. Your need is my
justice"), by making the tax system more equitable, by improving the state's roads, by overhauling the system of education.

But he also plays the political game with gusto, retaining
as his state auditor a man who has been guilty of widespread
graft, using "that scum down in the Legislature," and merci-

lessly putting down the opposition. Having the benefit of a carefully organized "research department," he is able to obtain "dirt" on any who try to upset him, the Congressman Petits and even the respected Judge Irwin. The Lincolnesque country lawyer undergoes a change in the face of "occupational corrosion."

Willie survives an attempted impeachment, the loss of upright supporters like Hugh Miller, and the scheme of his rival MacMurfee to bring him low by means of a scandal involving his son. But at the height of his career he is assassinated by the patrician doctor Adam Stanton. Stanton's ostensible reason for the slaying is his discovery of an affair between Stark and his sister Anne, but behind that lies a clash of attitudes toward life, the pragmatist Stark conflicting with the idealist Stanton.

This conflict throws into relief a part of the author's thesis that neither extreme pragmatism nor extreme idealism provides the proper approach to the complex business of living. Much can be said for both attitudes, to be sure. Stark, the practical politician and thus one who "pours out swill" to the people and who can recognize the politician's fundamental law of "gimme" and who uses blackmail methods and who, though unfaithful to his wife, makes sure that homey family pictures keep appearing in the newspapers, yet performs good deeds and gives his state better leadership—so Warren seems to feel—than it has had in the past.

Stark himself believes that the good and bad in life are inextricably mixed, and that good *can* come out of evil— and often does. Jack Burden attempts to illustrate the point:

155

a sonnet is not less good because it is concerned with illicit passion. Stark accepts the fact that one must often "do business" in order to arrive at what is "right" and that an abstract idealism such as that of Dr. Stanton seldom accomplishes a great deal. You make up the good as you go along, says the practical governor.

On the other hand, Stanton would plead for moral absolutes, for the permanence of principles. These he can put into practice in medicine, but perhaps not in politics and other areas. The surgeon may remain detached, even when performing an operation, but such pristine isolation is possible only for the very few.

According to Jack Burden, the position of neither man is wholly tenable; in fact, Adam Stanton as "man of idea" and Willie Stark as "man of fact" are doomed to destroy each other because each is incompatible "with the terrible division of their age."

What position should one take then? This is the question that in the last analysis concerns author Warren, and one which he poses through the book's principal figure Jack Burden. Throughout much of the novel Burden assumes the role of the detached cynic. Although, like Adam Stanton, he had once been an idealist—"a brass-bound idealist in college"—he had found this attitude to be "unreal." Family problems, graduate study, and newspaper experience had all, in one way or another, disillusioned him. For some time his answer is the "Great Sleep," an attitude of complete non-involvement. Although affected by his graduate research on Cass Mastern and by the latter's belief that ". . . it may be that only by the suffering of the innocent does God affirm that men are brothers, and brothers in his Holy Name," Jack shrugs the positive implications aside. He then deliberately enmeshes himself in politics—serving as a "legman" for Boss Stark, though knowing him to be more charlatan than hero.

In the political arena Burden can hardly help growing more cynical, having, for example, to expose his old family friend (and actually his father) Judge Irwin, and to witness the antics of political hangers-on such as Byram White and Tiny Duffy. Analyzing his feelings, he juxtaposes himself with Adam Stanton, contrasting the latter's existence, as a scientist, on finding things tidy, with his own belief, as a historian, that humans are and always have been a complicated mixture of good and bad.

Burden's cynicism reaches an extreme degree when he discovers that his own true love, Anne Stanton, is involved in an affair with Governor Stark. His reaction is to see life as nothing but the "Great Twitch" and man with little control over his destiny. By the time we understand the pattern we are in, he ruminates, it is too late to break out of the box. After Stark's death and the accession to power of Tiny Duffy (who is sure that Jack will work for him even though knowing that he was actually responsible for Stark's assassination), Jack realizes where his fatalistic nihilism has led him. Duffy and he both adore the Great Twitch, and they look alike.

This recognition shocks him into a recovery and the assumption of a different attitude as the best way to cope with life. One must accept the presence of both good and evil in the world, facing the often sad "truth," but not necessarily falling into a negative course of action as a consequence. The world, as Cass Mastern had said, resembles an enormous spider web, with everyone involved with everyone, and everyone touched by both good and evil. Man cannot escape the contamination, as Adam Stanton unconsciously thought, and retreat to pure idea, nor to the suspension of action represented in the Big Sleep, but the alternative need not be Willie Stark's unrestrained will either. The alternative is action modified by natural necessity but controlled by moral vision. The good man, learning from history as well as from the present moment, realizes that he must "help worldly decency conspire with unworldly truth"[2] in order to make the future palatable.

Jack has recognized responsibility, then, the responsibility of a human being involved in the "convulsion of the world." He perceives "greatness" in Willie Stark along with the "ungreatness," and that encourages more tolerance. He benefits from coming to an understanding of his mother, a woman with a greater capacity for love than he had been willing to grant. He also learns from his nominal father, the religiously-oriented Ellis Burden. Mr. Burden declares that evil is an index of God's glory and power. It had to be, so that the creation of *good* might be the index of man's glory and power. "But by God's help. By His help and in His Wisdom." Jack "accommodates" to this and thus escapes the "Great Twitch" and the denial of individual responsibility, and ends in an assertion—not rosily optimistic—of faith.

And so Warren's theme—posited in the epigraph from Dante at the beginning, "By curse of theirs man is not so lost that eternal love may not return, so long as hope retaineth aught of green"—is explicated. Man, if beset with

<hr />

[2] Thorp, *op. cit.*, 254.

the curse of evil, must have the will to hope and work for salvation, whatever the agony. As Cass Mastern sought to trace the slave girl maliciously sold down the river by Annabel Trice, as Ellis Burden endeavored to rehabilitate the disturbed fallen aerialist (a *try* at restoring Humpty Dumpty), as even Willie Stark tried to establish a "taint-free" hospital, so Jack Burden will accept the spotted past and strive for an unblemished future, in any event acting responsibly and humanely. History may be morally neutral, but man is not.

The foregoing discussion of the thesis of *All the King's Men* has suggested a shift in emphasis in the novel from the "king" to his "man." Certainly the study of an authoritarian personality seems a less central concern to the author than a study of a man's achieving self-fulfillment through self-recognition. Yet the two "studies" are deftly intertwined both structurally and thematically, the spider web world being seen for the most part against the vivid background of statehouse politics, and, as the narrator reminds us. ". . . the story of Willie Stark and the story of Jack Burden [being] in one sense, one story." The upper middle-class boy from Burden's Landing and the lower middle-class boy from an upcountry farm come together to demonstrate Warren's philosophy of interaction. The public world of politics is created by the author as a frame for the individual's private search for knowledge, for an understanding of his responsibility to his society and to himself.

In keeping with his thesis of the unfathomable intertwinings of guilt and innocence, Warren offers no all-black or all-white characters, at least, among the principals. Jack Burden, Lucy and Willie Stark, Sadie Burke, Anne and

Adam Stanton, and Judge Irwin assume very human proportions.

Willie Stark's cynical manipulation of the "slaves down at the legislature" is tempered by his genuine love for the "rednecks" of the country. Lucy Stark's perhaps too pharisaical view of life fights against her affection for her husband. Adam Stanton's many virtues are balanced by his too simpleminded morality and surrender to violence. Jack Burden, in particular, seems a very complex assortment of good and bad impulses. Anne Stanton may be the exception to this pattern of realistic characterization, she being too much the "golden girl." But even this conception becomes acceptable when we realize that she is being viewed through the eyes of a lover, who seldom manages to be impartial about her.

Warren makes a notable success of his two leading figures. Willie Stark very believably combines a dictatorial nature with his man-with-a-mission role. Flawed by his avid taste for power and willingness to use corruption to effect his ends, he is partially redeemed by his concern for the masses and his honesty about himself. A mixed man, but squarely in touch with the realities of everyday life, and seeking to soften these when possible by the application of "limited good." Jack Burden, as has been shown, undergoes a change in the course of the novel, from a cynical, ironic, discontented state to a position of synthesis, a mean between moral absolutism and pragmatic flexibility, and thus achieves contentment, if not wild ecstasy. This change is made very plausible, the escape from the vacuum of Burden's Landing to a feeling of engagement, the education in the political sphere, teaching, finally, that honor and love are not false qualities, that expediency and rationalization do not excuse all actions, that humans must accept full moral responsibility for their own conduct.

Technically speaking, the novel possesses many virtues. Its structural pattern, the double biography of Willie Stark and Jack Burden, is neatly established, and deftly maintained by the intermingling of a reporting of current events with flashbacks to the past. The use of retrospection adroitly supplies helpful background, peels back layer after layer of experience, and dramatizes the nature of what is happening to the principals.

Retrospective presentation also fits Warren's general theory about Time—a theory which runs throughout the book—that the past constantly impinges on the present and conditions the future. From the story of Cass Mastern, set well back in the past, Jack Burden learns of the intermixture of good and evil (Mastern's adultery and expiation). From the story of his mother, the scholarly attorney, and Judge Irwin, set in the recent past, Jack absorbs a similar lesson. Concluding that, "if you could accept the past you might hope for the future, for only out of the past can you make the future," he is prepared to go, with his wife Anne, "out of history into history and the awful responsibility of Time."

Warren tells his tale by means of a first person narrator, Jack Burden, and a happy arrangement this is, for it promotes a desirable narrator-reader intimacy, a proper informality of tone, and a solid perspective from which to view the events in the story. Remaining in the forefront (except during the unfolding of the Cass Mastern inset story), Jack interests the reader in his own development and at the same time sets up an effective angle of vision on Willie Stark. Through Jack's appraising look at him, we can more readily see how Willie is "half right and half wrong." The autobiographical method lends itself well to flashbacks, too. If one occasionally wishes that Jack's "recalls" were more selective, he readily admits that they are "launched" in a natural manner.

Warren is careful to preserve the correct tone for the narrator, a slangy but also very literate newspaperman (*and ex-graduate student*). Thus, the blending of two distinct styles, dry reporting of the action and an almost lyrical introspection seems permissible. We begin colloquially and and simply—"To get there you follow Highway 58, going northeast out of the city, and it is a good highway"—but we then encounter:

> I had gone down to the slums and seen the old man, the not very tall man who had once been stocky but whose face now drooped in puffy gray folds beneath the gray hair, with the steel-rimmed spectacles hanging on the end of the nose, and whose shoulders thin now and snowed with dandruff, sagged down as with the pull of the apparently disjunctive, careful belly which made the vest of his black suit pop up above the belt and the slack-hanging pants.

References to Hesiod and Caedmon and Coleridge mingle with obscenities and homely jargon. The images may have an earthy exactness about them—"like wet concrete in a posthole," "as juiceless as an old sponge left out in the sun a long time," "as numb and expressionless as a brace of gray oysters on the half shell"—or they may be picturesque and elaborate—e.g., New Mexico as a land of "magnificent emptiness with a little white filling station flung down on the sand like a sun-bleached cow skull by the trail." The diction also varies, from the colloquial "goose gumption" and "city-hall slob" to more fanciful phrasing, as "bone-white house," "spinner of smoke," "gossamer cord."

The Southern setting in the novel is vividly created, too. In the opening pages we see the "vitriolic, arsenical green of cotton rows" and the "violent, metallic, throbbing blue of the sky" and are immediately caught up in the Louisiana back-country atmosphere. The shabby farms and Negro shacks of this region are contrasted with the lovely ante-bellum mansions in Burden's Landing on the Gulf, as is the disreputable crib district with the garish governor's mansion in the state capital. We are made particularly aware of the Southern atmosphere of almost perpetual intense heat, which causes people to drip and their passions to rise, at political rallies, hotel-room conclaves, or legislative sessions.

One senses, in short, a thoroughly accomplished writer at work in *All the King's Men*. Warren, gifted in the solidity of specification, briskly describes an offbeat character like Sugar Boy, Stark's bodyguard, or a home such as the prim farm to which Lucy Stark withdraws, or the political atmos-phere surrounding the "courthouse clique." He deftly alter-nates thoughtful passages of reflection with satiric observa-tions and bits of humor, each expression of mood in keep-ing with the cynical-sensitive Jack Burden. Strong in speech and flow of action, and lucid in the exposition of his theme, Warren, one concludes, stays in control of his material at all times and produces a book of lasting appeal.

A little more political and a little less philosophical is Edwin O'Connor's *The Last Hurrah,* an artfully told story of one of the last of the big-city bosses, Frank Skeffington, operating in his Boston bailiwick. Described as a shrewd but charming rogue by author O'Connor, Skeffington serves as the very model of a model boss, receiving far more commendation than dispraise. Although probably unwilling to sanction the tactics of Boss Tweed and his successors like Kelly and Pendergast and Hague or even the supposed model for his Skeffington, James Michael Curley, O'Connor does gently bemoan the passing of the institution of "bossism."

Because it brings to life the boss figure, Frank Skeffington, the novel successfully dramatizes the theme of the demise of this political phenomenon. The central personage is seen as a human being, neither black nor white, rather, a most interesting shade of gray. In the first place, his physical attributes appear in his favor, recommending him both as a man and as a politician. He possesses a handsome face and fine presence, is carefully, though not ostentatiously, groomed, and speaks with great fluency, his Irish folksiness mingling with classical invective and "allowable erudition." Superficial attributes these, it should be noted; even the "allowable erudition" represents a decidedly shallow veneer of culture, Skeffington quoting from "The House by the Side of the Road" more often than from "Adonais," and in either event only to reproduce the elocutionary value of the poems. Still, his oratory is masterly, whether it is bland clichés for a huge open-air rally or a neat elaboration of a comparison between commuting businessmen and migratory fowl for an Audubon Society luncheon.

As a political figure Skeffington is immeasurably aided

by this impressive appearance and "gift of gab"; he is also aided by his ownership of a "grand heart" (his possession of which even his rival Charley Hennessey will grant), evident in his genuine concern for the well-being of the city of Boston and for the well-being of his constituents. To him the city owes its first substantial slum-clearing program. One has to credit him with wit, intelligence, and vast powers of cajolery also, an ability to placate the Portuguese stevedores, to win over the Italian laborers, and of course to delight his fellow Irishmen—most of them.

On the other hand, Frank Skeffington is a "crook" (as his rival Charley Hennessey will also grant), one who contravenes the law, permits graft and wasteful spending, and indulges in various methods of filling his own pockets. He can, in fact, be very dishonest—extracting money from the eminent banker Norman Cass by playing upon the vanity of his stupid son, or selling out his political supporter Camaratta. A cynical, outrageous old crook, as Edgar Burbank says, yet "simpatico."

The portrayal of Skeffington is skillfully built up largely through the opinions which others entertain about him, Roger Sugrue, the cardinal, Charley Hennessey, Nathaniel Gardiner, Festus Garvey, Monsignor Burke—some very much for, some very much against, some divided in their feeling. We also see him as he sees himself, and that is a surprisingly detached view. Throughout the novel, too, the public view of the character is balanced by the private view, the latter being that of Adam Caulfield, Skeffington's nephew. Caulfield observes his uncle's loneliness after the loss of his wife, the disappointment in his son and the unhappiness of his early life. At the same time Caulfield knows of his public activity, in fact, follows him on the campaign trail, and can react to that side of the person as well. He obviously feels—and makes the reader feel—that his uncle is an extraordinarily complex person.

Both as a person and as a boss Frank Skeffington is arresting. In the latter role he functions as the head of a tight organization, supported by his trusted lieutenants Weinberg and Gorman, then by the ward bosses, and so on down to the precinct leader and the voter. The "boss" keeps in touch with every rung, including the lowest, that of the people. These he learns about through an enormous correspondence, and through his habit of receiving a daily stream of visitors at his home or office. Distrusting any shortcuts to the electorate like television appearances, he goes to his constituents in person, attending ward dances and wakes, rallies and birthday celebrations. Skeffington utilizes the paternalistic system, acting as the "tribal chieftain" for the Irish, smoothly looking after their affairs and those of other ethnic groups as well. Each has a vote to bestow!

Surprisingly, though, Frank Skeffington loses power in the course of the novel, being defeated in the mayoralty election by the young figurehead McCluskey (he of the "let's-go-to-mass-together-on-Sunday voice"), and his loss is symbolic, O'Connor surmises, of the passing of the boss system from American politics. One of the novel's characters attributes the downfall of Skeffington to the social revolution instituted by Franklin D. Roosevelt, social security, unemployment insurance, and the like taking the place of paternalistic handouts.

It should also be remembered, however, that Skeffington was operating in a diminishing market, in Boston, at least. The young Irish felt remote from the racial-spokesman appeal, having been away from home, and subjected to different influences at Harvard or even at Boston College. Only the old and perhaps some of the middle-aged still shared with Skeffington the "ould sod" bond. The Irishman's status in Boston was changing.[3] This factor, added to the Rooseveltian welfare state, the perennial desire for a change of leaders and some concerted opposition to the authoritarian rule of Skeffington, brought about his defeat.

Although admitting that the "boss" system has fallen into disrepute—and probably should, since it contains many evils—O'Connor obviously regrets the departure from the scene of types such as Frank Skeffington. "Unique," says young Jack Mangan, and "miles ahead of the rest." A "great rogue," the proper Bostonian lawyer Nathaniel Gardiner admits, but, he adds, a most capable man, and certainly not a nonentity like the generation of ciphers coming to the fore.

In elaborating upon its sketch of Frank Skeffington, *The Last Hurrah* inserts a vast amount of authentic and fascinating detail about "inside politics." A host of political figures, colorfully and realistically drawn, throng the pages of the novel: Charley Hennessey, Mother Garvey, Nutsy Mc-

---

[3] Eric McKitrick, in his article "The Study of Corruption," describes how the whole question of social mobility affects the role of the political boss. See Eric L. McKitrick, "The Study of Corruption," *Political Science Quarterly*, Vol. 72 (December, 1957), 513–14.

For the Boston situation in particular, one should see also George Goodwin, Jr., "The Last Hurrahs: George Apley and Frank Skeffington," *The Massachusetts Review*, Vol. 1, (Spring, 1960), 461–71.

Grath, Ditto Boland, "political advance man" Cuke Gillen, "repeater voter" Footsie McEntee. Observations about the conduct of politics—". . . all successful political activity was based on *quid pro quo*," reformers "mow down half their own side"—crop up with frequency, and the political performances like candidate McCluskey's TV interview, with the Irish setter hired for the occasion and planted in the living room as a vote-getting prop, are many.

O'Connor carefully outlines the intricacies of the political campaign. The "boss" stages the operation most precisely: procuring the necessary finances (partly by his long-standing system of tithes); arranging each gathering down to the last detail (Colonel Reuben Ballou, Civil War survivor, is trotted out to all the rallies): talking at tea parties, open-air meetings, banquets, private houses; timing the sequence of events most rigidly; always, in fact, exhibiting tactical skill (the delayed entrances, the nodding, bowing, responding by name but never quite pausing) in handling the voting public.

Along with the pronounced political flavor, a strong sense of local color emanates from the novel. The Bostonian, at least, feels very much at home. O'Connor distinguishes among the principal "racial" elements of the city, the Irish, the Italians, and the old stock, or "proper Bostonian" group, living together in an always uneasy amalgam.

Much is made of the Irish in particular, and of their colorful folkways—Knocko Minihan's tax-supported wake, the professional mourner, Delia Boylan, the eccentricities of Charley Hennessey, the storytelling of Ditto Boland done in his inimitably "intricate narrative style." The novel even has a *roman à clef* appeal, the "knowing" reader identifying Skef-

fington with James M. Curley, the cardinal with the late
Cardinal O'Connell, the newspaper with the *Boston Herald*,
McCluskey with John Hynes, and Norman Cass, Jr., with
Russell Codman. Of course, he might go completely awry
in his identifications. Mr. Curley himself could not quite
make up his mind as to whether Skeffington was modeled
after him or not.

O'Connor tells his tale in an easy manner, tidily mixing
exposition with dramatic scenes (such as the Camaratta-
Garvey conflict), dialogue with reverie. The novel is appro-
priately structured in four divisions, the first devoted to
Skeffington's decision to run for office once again, the second
to the subsurface maneuvering in the early stages of the
campaign, the third to the final week, the fourth to the loss
of the election and Skeffington's illness and death. The drama
of the campaign, climaxing in the election night scene, during which the boss's hangers-on, loyal but apprehensive,
watch the gradual alteration of the balance of votes, presents
an exciting format. Interest continues through the denouement, the recapitulation of the final days of the boss, with
their underscoring of the "I'd do it again" theme.

Despite the underlying mood of poignance, the novel is
enlivened by many delightful humorous touches. The reader
chuckles at Festus Garvey's using his ancient crone of a
mother an as effective campaign device, at Skeffington's big
air-conditioned voice eulogizing Eddie McLoughlin so ful-
somely that he was rendered totally unrecognizable to his
widow, at Ditto Boland's wanting Skeffington's grave to be
both a shrine and a sepulchral family picnic ground, and at
political reporter "Mattress" Mulroony, who, wishing to

keep his reporting objective, never visited city hall, in fact, never left his bed. The appearances of Charley Hennessey, dacron cap, tape recorder and all, the folklorish tales about Father Fahey and the Reverend Mr. Payne, the "ghastly punitive repasts" of tightwad publisher Amos Force, the macabre conversational exchange between Delia Boylan and the undertaker also provoke spontaneous laughter. In author O'Connor one encounters the proverbial Irish wit.

A clear and facile style is also an asset of the novel. The author mimics adeptly (Cass, Jr.'s lisp, a "thimply thuperb old thloop"), reproduces the Irish dialect with exactitude, employs well-turned characterizing phrases—the "fruity pomposity" of Ditto Boland or the "whinny" of waspish "Miss Lonelyhearts" Burbank. Etching in acid vignettes—of "reet, reet" Fats Citronella; Francis Skeffington, Jr., a "very old undergraduate" type; Roger Sugrue, the self-made lingerie-maker ("Success among the undergarments had given him confidence")—O'Connor animates his characters with sprightly succinctness and only rarely strikes a false note. If the penny-pinching newspaper editor is an unbelievable caricature, not so his boss, the irascible old-line Bostonian, Amos Force, and not so most of the participants in the novel. Selecting his words meticulously, O'Connor "catches" the smooth speech of Skeffington ("an elaborate web of tactful response") and the easy chatter of young matron Nancy Mangan. He plays upon words, introduces the paradoxical phrase ("compulsory high spirits"), and the graphic figure of speech ("the size of the plurality is like the color of a raincoat in a typhoon"). Interesting to observe, too, is his reliance upon military terms like "verbal infighting" or "the little bands of political guerillas roaming the corridors of City Hall," fitting images for political proceedings which so often amount to "warfare."

Although *The Last Hurrah* deserves praise on many counts, its humor and felicitous style, its well-made quality and bona fide political atmosphere, the book is chiefly distinguished by its presentation of a protagonist of stature. As we follow the career of the "governor," learning to admire his "good-humored audacity" and compassion, if also to scoff at his occasionally merciless tactics, we recognize the intricacies of the figure, and we leave him, feeling a large measure of admiration. The portrait of Frank Skeffington decisively increases the value of *The Last Hurrah* as a literary effort. Not to be forgotten is its effect on the book's political issue either. Instructing us as to the difficulties involved in ascertaining the truth with regard to men in public life, the sketch persuades us to think twice about the subject of "bosses" and possibly to subject our previous commitments to revision.

As wholeheartedly devoted to political matters as *The Last Hurrah*, Allen Drury's *Advise and Consent* comprehensively examines the workings of the United States Senate and the Washington political scene in general. The author puts the Capitol Hill environment squarely before us, ranging from the Senate lunch room to the Supreme Court tribunal.

In the course of his exhaustive, reasonably accurate, and often fascinating account, one sees senators of all descriptions, the charming but ruthless President, the amiable Vice-President, the back-slapping national chairman, Chaplain

Carney Birch, the ancient but shrewd Speaker of the House, Supreme Court justices, Washington hostesses like Dolly Harrison, foreign diplomats, etc. Scenes are played out in senatorial offices, the White House, fashionable drawing rooms, the Senate chamber. In the process we become well informed about political personages—"the mainly amiable gentlemen of the Senate" and the State Department people with their "fairly seedy youthfulness"—and about their work, realistically described as a "bargaining between ideals and ambitions."

The central issue, which brings all the ramifications of the political picture into focus, concerns the deposing of the current Secretary of State Howie Sheppard and the question of his replacement. The leading candidate, Bob Leffingwell, mid-twentieth century America's representative "Equivocal Man" and seemingly highly unsuited for the post, has many supporters, including the President, and very nearly secures the appointment.

Involved in the debate are such leading senatorial figures as Majority Leader Bob Munson, the powerful Southern senator Seab Cooley, the "western star" Senator Brigham Anderson, and the reactionary junior senator from Wyoming, Fred Van Ackerman. Supreme Court Justice Davis, desirous of the Leffingwell nomination, is willing to blackmail Senator Anderson, who has been influentially opposing the nomination. The President utilizes Davis's scandalous information, employing "hatchet-man" Van Ackerman to disseminate it, while Senator Munson—for a time—stands idly by.

Gossip, speculation and behind-the-hand talk run riot, often aided by the "press pack on the prowl," with Brigham

Anderson's suicide as the unhappy result. This misfortune so shocks the Senate that it passes a resolution of censure against the demagogic Van Ackerman and arranges a perpetual "implacable ostracism." But the Leffingwell nomination remains a hot issue. The President continues to finagle for his confirmation, and the press and the country back him up, as well as most of the foreign ambassadors. The situation is at length resolved, with the Senate refusing "consent," the President fortuitously dying and thus allowing the Vice-President-become-President to advance a more suitable candidate, Senator Orrin Knox, who is quickly endorsed.

In effecting a solution to this appointment problem, Drury tips the scale in favor of the basically clear-seeing Senate, more to be trusted than the "troops," the masses. He thus contends that the "ancient mores of the lodge" are essentially sound, that the Senate, if not perfect, has the vitality and integrity of free men. For every Fred Van Ackerman ("every once in a while the electoral process tosses to the top someone smart and glib and evil, without basic principle, without basic character, and without restraints"), one can find an Orrin Knox or a Stanley Danta, men of honesty, candor, determination and tart integrity. And, if this be the Age of the Shoddy, the Age of the Shrug, still, the great ideals triumph in the end. The reader has his reservations, however; power and ambition hold sway, and at best uneasy compromises result.

The novel concentrates, in fact, upon the theme of power, a power that warps and corrodes the politicians motivated by a desire for it and taints political life with corruption. The picture of Washington given in *Advise and Consent* would certainly have struck the Founding Fathers as the epitome of a corrupt society. The Senate may show the "vitality of free men" while still not necessarily serving the true ends of popular government. Selfish motivation and the "necessary workaday hypocrisy" militate against this. Because people are ultimately good, so Drury insists, the point of convergence of their self-seeking interests will ultimately be good, too. Unfortunately, the conclusion does not follow precisely from the premise, and even the premise might be regarded as suspect. Drury himself describes many, many individuals who would not be "ultimately good." When a Supreme Court justice will indulge in blackmail and when the President of the United States will "play along," the picture is black, the corruption there.

The Washington scene has a decidedly "jungl-y" air, then, in *Advise and Consent*, but it also seems, sad to say, authentically reproduced. The tan, marble-paneled fish bowl that is the Senate chamber rises before us at the beginning of the novel and remains very much in our minds throughout. In this "cave of the winds" the senators argue for their pet appropriations, debate furiously on controversial issues, and engage in various parliamentary maneuvers to secure advantage for themselves. The reader observes in the foreground the majority and minority leaders, the party whips and the presiding officer, and in the background the "mimeograph senators," the newly arrived or the passé. Whether in front or in back, they play a rough game, underneath the backslaps and handshakes and noble speeches. Votes are rounded up on the basis of *quid pro quo,* colleagues in disfavor are kept off the good committees, and the incompetent or unobliging are subjected to the little cruelties of parliamentary technique which will razor a man down to political nothingness inch by inch.

Of course, neither everything nor everybody is so pejoratively treated, for, as Drury reminds us toward the end of the novel, politics contains as much good as evil, the American system of government permitting "freedom" to do right as well as wrong. One does observe capable men in the Senate, one does listen to perceptive speeches on the floor (as Senator Munson's careful reminder of the legislative branch's check on the power of the executive), and one does hear intelligent and principled statements in committee hearings and caucuses. Men such as Vice-President Hudson grow in stature, and even adroit and "feudist" politicians like Senator Cooley have an impressive concept of the United States which they do not wish to see damaged.

Part of the book's vividness stems from its susceptibility to being read as a *roman à clef*. Certainly there is some amusement in seeing the late Senator Taft in Orrin Knox; Krishna Menon in the Indian ambassador "K.K.," a temporizing and excessively bland figure; Harry Truman in Harley Hudson; possibly Franklin Roosevelt in the President (the voice with the "happy lilt," accompanying the "toss of the head"); and surely the late Senator McCarthy in Fred Van Ackerman. But, as Irving Kristol remarks,[4] the familiar faces are often attached to odd bodies and given unfamiliar roles, e.g.,

[4] Irving Kristol, "Strange Gods on Capitol Hill" (Review of *Advise and Consent*), *The Reporter*, Vol. 21 (November 12, 1959), 38.

Van Ackerman as a reverse McCarthy, and the searching for identities should remain an idle, if rather captivating, game.

Although the narration retains a down-to-mud reality from beginning to end, questions arise about the author's handling of the political issue even so. Would a Supreme Court justice be so morally weak as "Tommy" Davis? Would a President—especially one who had supposedly "dreamed great dreams and done great things"—resort to lies, deceit, and blackmail? Could Senator Munson salve his conscience as easily as he does or be welcomed back so quickly into the fold? Would so many astute individuals continue to support Leffingwell for the secretaryship even after his uncritical penchant for peace and his fuzzy ideas about foreign policy had become well known? How plausible is the possibility that a mass movement could be started among Americans with the slogan, "We would rather crawl to Moscow on our knees than perish under a bomb?" *Advise and Consent* stretches our credulity in too many instances. Drury's conclusion, too, that the "good" will eventually prevail, does not, alas, seem warranted by the facts presented. It is the image of evil that lingers on.

The novel troubles one particularly, however, because it affords only qualified aesthetic satisfaction. Despite the popular acclaim and rather extensive critical approval that have been bestowed upon it, it must be considered a flawed performance. It cannot claim, for one thing, any very careful characterization, any progression beyond the one-dimensional figure. Cord Meyer rightly complains that Drury conjures up no "fully imagined and complexly motivated human beings confronting with believable anguish the hard choices

176

that practical politics frequently present."[5] The utterly stereotyped foreign diplomats, the English, French, and Russian ambassadors tend to prove the point, and so, too, do many of the United States officials.

Once Senator August's vacillating nature is established, he is forever defined, and the same may be said of "spiteful" Senator Richardson, or "firmly quiet" Senator Adams, or "jolly" Senator Eastwood, or "sardonic" Senator Fry. Even the principals—the smooth-talking Bob Leffingwell or the calculatingly charming President—have a "humors" quality about them. Both Seab Cooley and Orrin Knox, despite the many pages devoted to them, seem to be "characters," too much the colorful, idiosyncratic personality type to be "complexly motivated." Lafe Smith, though humanized by his shifting moods, is still too "tagged" (as the gay blade of the Senate) to be wholly credible, and, conversely, Bob Munson, for all his prominence in directing the book's action, remains shadowy and unconvincing. One exception to the Meyer complaint may be cited, Senator Brigham Anderson. His is a moving portrayal, with the "private fortress" as well as the public façade unveiled, and the section of the novel devoted to him is much the most impressive part of *Advise and Consent*.

The novel does possess "impressive parts," it is only fair to say, author Drury displaying a knack for spinning an engrossing narrative pattern and charging a scene with drama. The reader will not quickly forget the acerbic give-and-take of the committee hearings, the suicide sequence, the Van

[5] Cord Meyer, Jr., Review of *Advise and Consent*, *The Kenyon Review*, Vol. 22 (Spring, 1960), 328.

Ackerman censure vote. At times, to be sure, the drama verges on melodrama, the domestic poignance on sentimentality, but the reality of the Anderson marriage strain or of Senator Knox's battle with his presidential ambition cannot be denied.

Drury holds his lengthy narrative together, too, by a compressed time span and by his concentration on the secretary of state succession question, which remains in the forefront throughout the unfolding of the four major blocks of the narrative, the "stories" of Senators Munson, Cooley, Anderson, and Knox. Yet, *Advise and Consent,* like most long novels, is simply too long, and its orderly structure cannot hide this defect. The author recounts at too great length the backgrounds of the central senators and the details of senatorial committee activity. He inserts two superfluous romances which we would willingly forego and further distracts us by his intermittent prose poems to Washington and some too obvious foreshadowing passages. His panoramic view device is overdone also; the constant series of snippet scenes grows to resemble nothing so much as plain padding.

Drury's style causes the greatest uneasiness, veering as it does from rhapsodic overwriting to limping journalese and seldom if ever achieving a supple, natural flow. Spotted with *Time* jargon and press conference syntax, as Irving Kristol crisply says,[6] the writing is marred by triteness of diction, too, and by some heavy-handed attempts at satire. The author, relying heavily on dialogue throughout the book, occasionally inflicts highly unrealistic conversations upon us,

---

[6] Kristol, "Strange Gods on Capitol Hill," (Review of *Advise and Consent*), *The Reporter*, Vol. 21 (November 12, 1959), 38.

e.g., the exchanges between the wives of the British and French ambassadors, or the coy love passages between Mrs. Harrison and Senator Munson. He permits himself too many hackneyed phrases ("rat race," "hand on helm," "get on my horse"), too many awkward expressions ("plans firmed up"), too many cataloguing sentences, and, on the other hand, too few figures of speech, too few well-turned and memorable sentences. His is undeniably a less professional talent than that of Warren or O'Connor.

Advise and Consent still deserves to be called a "successful illustration" of the political novel genre, however. The Washington phenomena are punctiliously ranged before us —the Senate hearing in front of the television cameras, the lavish and gossipy party, the strategy sessions of the inner circle, the incessant pursuit of senators by eager newsmen —and the role-of-the-Senate theme is thoroughly analyzed. It is disheartening, of course, to feel that Drury has demonstrated once again how in America political figures place ambition above conscience, and disheartening to realize that corruption remains the traditional thesis. Yet one is grateful that Drury has brought knowledgeability to his examination of American politics and a fair measure of competence as well.

☆

CHAPTER X

Conclusion

THE American political novel has enjoyed a long and lively history, having flourished—sometimes in an approximate form—from the latter days of the eighteenth century to the present. If it has concentrated on a "narrow scope of experience," often exhibited a "limited philosophy,"[1] and seldom achieved genuine artistic success, yet the genre has won more than the "incidental position"[2] John Chamberlain accords it, by virtue of its continued popular appeal down through the years.

Usually taking as a starting point a series of actual—and almost always seamy—happenings, writers from H. H. Brackenridge to Jerome Weidman have fictionized about the American political arena, finding many elements of drama and the interplay of human passion therein. With the background of the legislative session or the campaign stump or even the Supreme Court robing room, they have described the political acts (not always the obvious ones like legislating) of the usually authoritarian and vibrant personalities who are the successful politicians, and in developing the genre they

[1] Walter F. Taylor, "Fiction and Social Debate," *Literary History of the United States* (ed. by Robert Spiller, *et al.*) (New York, The Macmillan Company, 1948), Vol. II, 987.

[2] John F. Chamberlain, *Farewell to Reform*, 177.

have provided a record of significant periods in American life and of the people who shaped them.

In the earliest era, "gentlemen" like Cooper, Tucker, and Kennedy commented on democracy-turned-demagoguery. Then came satires on big business control of politics, as the earlier aristocratic democracy changed into a plutocracy and the "gentleman" was relegated to the sidelines and to rather feeble pleading for civil service reform. Only a few of the clean-cut type threw themselves into the political maelstrom, and fewer survived the whirlpool. Farmers and laborers protested big business control as well, the former staging the agrarian revolt, which political novelists such as Hamlin Garland selected as their subject matter, and the latter really having to wait until the 1930's, when the proletarian novel gave them their innings at last.

For a long while the "radical" found no role in the political novel (Cooper was not interested in the Sam Adams type), and for almost as long women played no part—not until Garland, in *A Spoil of Office*, made literary capital of the colorful figure of Mary Ellen "Raise-less-corn-and-more-hell" Lease, a leader in the Populist movement.

Twentieth century political fiction has come to embrace all sorts of topics and all sorts of characters, in novels ranging from the muckraking *The Grafters* (1904) to the comic *Haunch, Paunch and Jowl* (1923) to the analytical *The Middle of the Journey* (1947). Topics such as legislative corruption and bossism linger on, while those of disabled liberalism, the role of the United Nations (Allen Drury's *A Shade of Difference*, 1962), and the threat of the computer as a manipulator of mass opinion (Eugene Burdick's *The 480*, 1964) have been added. The gallery of political types has been augmented by the gangster, labor organizer, bemused radical, and that man-of-all-talents Upton Sinclair's remarkable Lanny Budd, while the big business mogul (giant to some, rascal to others), lobbyist, and hireling newspaperman remain. Indeed, the political novel has a "well demonstrated vitality as a literary form."[3]

Questions as to the literary merit of the type, and as to its influence remain, however. On the first count, as has become apparent in the course of our study, not very extravagant claims can be made. Technically, the novels—the run of them—display decided weaknesses. The simplest structural patterns (usually the biographical sequence) are employed, and the plots invariably combine politics and romance, the latter "sop" appearing even in the most recent fiction. Although settings are well evoked—e.g., the exhausted anguish of the political campaign—the authors' styles incline toward the pedestrian. Their characters, too, function as mouthpieces rather than as flesh and blood creations and are either unduly idealized (the Robin Hood boss) or unduly denigrated. Nor are they studied as reflecting the ordered political philosophies of their creators. In other words, the themes of most political novels lack subtlety or depth, too often substituting for these mere rhetoric and propaganda.

Here is the "heart of the matter." The political novel is a purpose novel, a difficult form to "carry off," as novelists and critics alike have agreed. Some writers will boldly declare that the introduction of dogma into creative work is always

[3] Blotner, *op. cit.*, 94.

detrimental,[4] but others, pointing to a long and honorable body of work, including such as that of Tolstoy, sanction the presence of the didactic message. Admittedly, the dogma must be introduced unobtrusively, and without distortion or exaggeration, and the writer must think of his craft first:

> . . . it is not the class loyalties nor a Marxist background of a writer which can equip him for the difficult task of writing; he must possess the indispensable talent, command of his material, technical mastery. The writer is primarily a craftsman.[5]

Ideally, the writer knows whereof he speaks (is, in this case, not politically ignorant)—though not necessarily being a problem-solver—but at the same time remains responsible to his "humanness and his art."[6] It is still a difficult task to dramatize didacticism, however, and only a few of the political novelists succeed.

Do they succeed in delivering their message—artistically or otherwise—and in causing people to act upon this message? Do the novels, generating heat *and* illumination, cause the reader to go on the warpath? Generally speaking, no. Some of the novels have been widely read and have incited a greater interest in politics and a fuller understanding, and in no case has their interest been so ephemeral as that of newspaper or magazine articles. But reforms—often their *raison d'être*—have seldom proceeded directly, if at all, from

[4] Obed Brooks, "The Problem of the Social Novel," *Modern Language Quarterly*, Vol. 6 (Autumn, 1932), 79.

[5] Charles I. Glicksberg, "Proletarian Fiction in the United States," *Dalhousie Review*, Vol. 17 (April, 1937), 32.

[6] Wayne Burns, "The Novelist as Revolutionary," *Arizona Quarterly*, Vol. 7 (Spring, 1951), 27.

these fictions. Readers have been awakened but not pushed into action. The reason for the failure to rally round would seem to be simply this: the novelists have offered many broad generalities, few positive suggestions. They have mostly made an appeal to morality as the way to solve political problems, hoping to stir up the reforming zeal so characteristic of Americans and to prod them into being mindful of Cooper's injunction that it is "the duty of the citizen to reform and improve the character of his country."[7]

It is probably asking too much, however, to expect the political novelist to solve the problems. He is neither a political scientist, nor even an historian, never a political columnist and very rarely a practicing politician. To call upon him for more than a depiction of the hoopla and general ineffectiveness of the national nominating conventions—for a substitute means of insuring that the candidates are selected by the popular will—or to anticipate from him a prediction as to the effect of the changing role of the President in this modern era, is to be unreasonable.

Walter Rideout reminds us that the "function of the novel . . . is to make the reader aware. . . . A novel does not send its reader to the barricades or the altar, but rather enlarges his experience, makes him realize more fully the possibilities of the human being. The novel, whatever its formal ideology, is essentially a humanizing force."[8] And Joseph Blotner, speaking more specifically of the political novel genre, takes a similar tack: "If a novelist gains a reader's

[7] Quoted in Charles L. Sanford, "Classics of American Reform Literature," *American Quarterly*, Vol. 10 (Fall, 1958), 295.
[8] Walter Rideout, *op. cit.*, 289-90.

support for a cause, arouses his distaste for a course of action, or simply produces a reevaluation of previously accepted beliefs, his work has served as a political instrument."[9]

An interesting and provocative form of fiction, then, the political novel. Since it offers an insight into the nature of the always fascinating political being and of the society in which he lives, it contains a perennial lure, a lure which lingers even when the form turns into a ponderous morality play rather than the sparkling comedy of manners or the reflective disquisition it might be.

Sometimes, of course, the art and the analysis do blend, and the form turns out as it should. We have had, as proof of this, several excellent novels of politics—and there will be more.

[9] Blotner, *op. cit.*, 10.

☆

Bibliography

I. Primary Sources—the Novels

Adams, Henry. *Democracy*. 1882.

Adams, Samuel H. *Plunder*. 1948.

——. *Revelry*, 1926.

Atherton, Gertrude. *Senator North*. 1900.

Bacheller, Irving. *The Light in the Clearing*. 1917.

Basso, Hamilton. *Sun in Capricorn*. 1942.

Benson, Ramsey. *Hill Country*. 1928.

Brammer, William. *The Gay Place*. 1961.

Browne, Lewis. *See What I Mean*. 1943.

——. *Oh, Say, Can You See*. 1937.

Burdick, Eugene. *The 480*. 1964.

——. *The Ninth Wave*. 1956.

——, and Harvey Wheeler. *Fail-Safe*. 1962.

Burnett, Frances H. *Through One Administration*. 1881.

Burnett, W. R. *King Cole*. 1936.

Busch, Nevin. *The Hate Merchant*. 1953.

Chatterton, Ruth. *The Betrayers*. 1953.

Churchill, Winston. *Coniston*. 1906.

——. *Mr. Crewe's Career*. 1908.

Clune, Henry. *By His Own Hand*. 1952.

Cohen, Lester. *Coming Home*. 1945.

Cooper, James Fenimore. *The Crater*. 1847.

——. *The Monikins*. 1836.

——. *The Redskins*. 1846.

——. *The Ways of the Hour*. 1850.

Crawford, F. Marion. *An American Politician*. 1884.

Curtis, George William. *Trumps*. 1860.

Davis, Rebecca Harding. *John Andross*. 1874.

——. *Margaret Howth*. 1862.

DeForest, John W. *Honest John Vane*. 1875 (Monument Edition, 1960).

——. *Playing the Mischief*. 1875 (Monument Edition, 1961).

Denison, T. S. *An Iron Crown*. 1885.

Dillon, Mary. *The Leader*. 1906.

Dinneen, Joseph F. *Ward Eight*. 1936.

Dos Passos, John. *Chosen Country*. 1951.

——. *District of Columbia*. 1952.

Dreiser, Theodore. *The Titan*. 1914.

Drury, Allen. *Advise and Consent*. 1959.

——. *A Shade of Difference*. 1962.

Eggleston, Edward. *The Mystery of Metropolisville*. 1900.

Fairbank, Janet A. *The Lion's Den*. 1930.

——. *Rich Man, Poor Man*. 1936.

Fast, Howard. *The American*. 1946.

Fergusson, Harvey. *Capitol Hill*. 1923.

Flower, Elliott. *The Spoilsmen*. 1903.

Ford, Paul Leicester. *The Honorable Peter Stirling*. 1894.

Garland, Hamlin. *A Member of the Third House*. 1892.

——. *A Spoil of Office*. 1892.

Glasgow, Ellen. *The Voice of the People*. 1900.

Grant, Robert. *Unleavened Bread*. 1900.

Hackett, Francis. *The Senator's Last Night*. 1943.

Hamlin, Myra S. *A Politician's Daughter*. 1886.

Herrick, Robert. *The Memoirs of an American Citizen*. 1905.

Holland, Josiah G. *Sevenoaks*. 1875.

Horan, James D. *The Seat of Power*. 1965.

Hume, J. F. *Five Hundred Majority*. 1872.

Huston, McCready. *Dear Senator*. 1928.

Keenan, Henry. *The Money-Makers*. 1885.

Kennedy, John Pendleton. *Quodlibet*. 1840.

Kimbrough, Edward. *From Hell to Breakfast*. 1941.
Knebel, Fletcher and Charles W. Bailey. *Convention*. 1964.
Langley, Adria Locke. *A Lion Is In the Streets*. 1945.
Lewis, Alfred. *The Boss*. 1902.
———. *The President*. 1904.
Lewis, Sinclair. *It Can't Happen Here*. 1935.
Lippard, George. *The Empire City*. 1864.
Locke, David R. *The Demagogue*. 1891.
———. *A Paper City*. 1879.
Lush, Charles K. *The Autocrats*. 1901.
———. *The Federal Judge*. 1897.
Luther, Mark Lee. *The Henchman*. 1902.
Lynde, Francis. *The Grafters*. 1904.
Masters, E. L. *Children of the Market Place*. 1922.
Mayer, Martin. *Governor's Choice*. 1956.
McSpadden, J. Walker. *Storm Center*. 1947.
O'Connor, Edwin. *The Last Hurrah*. 1956.
O'Hara, John. *Ten North Frederick*. 1955.
Page, Thomas Nelson. *John Marvel, Assistant*. 1909.
Partridge, Bellamy. *Big Freeze*. 1948.
Paul, Elliott. *The Governor of Massachusetts*. 1942.
Paulding. James K. *Koningsmarke*. 1823.
———. *Westward Ho*. 1832.
Phillips, Elizabeth Stuart. *The Silent Partner*. 1871.
Phillips, David Graham. *The Cost*. 1904.
———. *The Deluge*. 1905.
———. *George Helm*. 1912.
———. *Golden Fleece*. 1903.
———. *The Great God Success*. 1901.
———. *Joshua Craig*. 1909.
———. *Light-Fingered Gentry*. 1907.
———. *The Plum Tree*. 1905.
Poole, Ernest. *The Harbor*. 1915.
Scaevola, Peter. *'68*. 1964.
Shapley, Rufus E. *Solid for Mulhooly*. 1881.

188

Shaw, Irwin. *The Troubled Air.* 1951.

Sinclair, Upton. *Boston.* 1928.

———. *The Jungle.* 1906.

Stribling, T. S. *The Sound Wagon.* 1935.

———. *These Bars of Flesh.* 1938.

Sylvester, Harry. *Moon Gaffney.* 1947.

Tarkington, Booth. *The Gentleman From Indiana.* 1899.

———. *In the Arena.* 1905.

Taylor, Henry J. *The Big Man.* 1964.

Thomas, Frederick W. *Clinton Bradshaw,* 1835.

Tourgee, Albion W. *A Fool's Errand.* 1879.

Train, Arthur. *Tassels on her Boots.* 1940.

Trilling, Lionel. *The Middle of the Journey.* 1947.

Tucker, Nathaniel B. *The Partisan Leader.* 1861.

Tully, Andrew. *Capitol Hill.* 1962.

———. *Supreme Court.* 1963.

Twain, Mark and Charles Dudley Warner. *The Gilded Age.* 1873.

Warren, Robert Penn. *All the King's Men.* 1946.

Wellman, Paul I. *The Walls of Jericho.* 1938.

Wendell, Barrett. *Rankell's Remains.* 1896.

Wharton, Edith. *The Fruit of the Tree.* 1907.

White, William Allen. *A Certain Rich Man.* 1909.

Whitlock, Brand. *Her Infinite Variety.* 1904.

———. *The Thirteenth District.* 1902.

———. *The Turn of the Balance.* 1907.

Wicker, Tom. *The Kingpin.* 1953.

Williams, Francis C. *J. Devlin, Boss.* 1901.

II. Secondary Sources—Books

Aaron, Daniel. *Men of Good Hope.* New York, Oxford University Press, 1951.

———. *Writers on the Left.* New York, Harcourt Brace & World, Inc., 1961.

Adams, Frederick, B., Jr. *Radical Literature in America*. Stamford, Connecticut, The Overbrook Press, 1939.

Adams, Samuel H. *Incredible Era*. Boston, Houghton Mifflin Co., 1939.

Allen, Frederick Lewis. *The Lords of Creation*. New York, London, Harper & Bros., 1935.

Blotner, Joseph. *The Political Novel*. Garden City, New York, Doubleday, 1955.

Bohner, Charles H. *Robert Penn Warren*. New York, Twayne Publishers, Inc., 1964.

Bolles, Blair. *Men of Good Intentions: Crisis of the American Presidency*. Garden City, New York, Doubleday, 1960.

Brooks, Van Wyck. *The Confident Years, 1885–1915*. New York, E. P. Dutton & Co., 1952.

———. *Emerson and Others*. New York, E. P. Dutton & Co., 1927.

Budd, Louis J. *Mark Twain: Social Philosopher*. Bloomington, Indiana, Indiana University Press, 1962.

Calverton, V. F. *The Liberation of American Literature*. New York, C. Scribner's Sons, 1932.

Cargill, Oscar, ed. *The Social Revolt: American Literature from 1884 to 1914*. New York, The Macmillan Co., 1933.

Casper, Leonard. *Robert Penn Warren, The Dark and Bloody Ground*. Seattle, Washington, University of Washington Press, 1960.

Chalmers, David M. *The Social and Political Ideas of the Muckrakers*. New York, The Citadel Press, 1964.

Chamberlain, John. *Farewell to Reform*. New York, Liveright, Inc., 1932.

Coan, Otis W. and Richard G. Lillard. *America in Fiction*. Palo Alto, California, Stanford University Press, 1941.

Commager, Henry Steele. *The American Mind*. New Haven, Yale University Press, 1950.

Cooper, Frederick T. *Some American Story Tellers*. New York, H. Holt & Co., 1911.

Curti, Merle. *The Growth of American Thought*. New York, London, Harper & Bros., 1943.

Dickinson, A. T., Jr. *American Historical Fiction*. New York, The Scarecrow Press, 1958.

DuBreuil, Alice J. *The Novel of Democracy in America*. Baltimore, J. H. Furst Co., 1923.

Eisinger, Chester E. *Fiction of the Forties*. Chicago & London, University of Chicago Press, 1963.

Faulkner, Harold U. *From Versailles to the New Deal*. New Haven, Yale University Press, 1950.

———. *Politics, Reform & Expansion, 1890–1900*. New York, Harper's, 1959.

———. *The Quest for Social Justice, 1898–1914*. New York, The Macmillan Co., 1931.

Filler, Louis. *Crusaders for American Liberalism*. New York, Harcourt Brace, 1950.

Fine, Nathan. *Labor and Farmer Parties in the United States*. New York, Rand School of Social Science, 1928.

Flory, Claude R. *Economic Criticism in American Fiction*. Philadelphia, University of Pennsylvania, 1936.

Flynn, Edward J. *You're the Boss*. New York, Viking Press, 1947.

Gabriel, Ralph H. *The Course of American Democratic Thought*. New York, The Ronald Press Co., 1940.

Goldman, Eric F. *The Crucial Decade, 1944–1955*. New York, Knopf, 1956.

———. *Rendezvous with Destiny*. New York, Knopf, 1952.

Gosnell, Harold F. *Grass Roots Politics*. Washington, American Council on Public Affairs, 1942.

Graham, George A. *Morality in American Politics*. New York, Random House, 1952.

Grimes, Alan P. *American Political Thought*. New York, H. Holt & Co., 1955.

Gurko, Leo. *The Angry Decade*. New York, Dodd, Mead, 1947.

Hartwick, Harry. *The Foreground of American Fiction*, New York, Cincinnati, American Book Co., 1934.

Hartz, Louis. *The Liberal Tradition in America*. New York, Harcourt Brace, 1955.

Hatcher, Harlan. *Creating the Modern American Novel*. New York, Farrar & Rhinehart, Inc. 1935.

Hicks, Granville. *The Great Tradition*. New York, The Macmillan Co., 1935.

Hofstadter, Richard. *The American Political Tradition*. New York, Knopf, 1948.

———. *The Age of Reform*. New York, Knopf, 1955.

Holbrook, Stewart H. *The Age of the Moguls*. Garden City, New York, Doubleday, 1954.

———. *Lost Men of American History*. New York, The Macmillan Co., 1946.

Hollingsworth, J. Rogers. *The Whirligig of Politics*. Chicago and London, University of Chicago Press, 1963.

Howe, Irving. *Politics and the Novel*. New York, Horizon Press, 1957.

Johnson, Tom. *My Story*. New York, B. W. Huebsch, 1913.

Johnson, Walter. *1600 Pennsylvania Ave*. Boston, Little, Brown, 1960.

Josephson, Matthew. *The President-Makers*. New York, Harcourt, Brace, 1940.

———. *The Robber Barons*. New York, Harcourt Brace, 1938.

Kane, Harnett, T. *Louisiana Hayride*. New York, W. Morrow & Co., 1941.

Kiplinger, W. M. *Washington Is Like That*. New York, Lonlon, Harper & Bros., 1942.

Kirkland, Edward C. *Business in the Gilded Age*. Madison, Wisconsin, University of Wisconsin Press. 1952.

Knight, Grant C. *American Literature and Culture*. New York, Ray Long and Richard R. Smith, Inc., 1932.

———. *The Strenuous Age in American Literature*. Chapel Hill, N. C., University of North Carolina Press, 1954.

Light, James F. *John William De Forest*. New York, Twayne Publishers, Inc., 1965.

Link, Arthur S. *American Epoch*. New York, Knopf, 1963 (2nd edition).

Luthin, Reinhard H. *American Demagogues, Twentieth Century*. Boston, Beacon Press, 1954.

Lynch, Denis T. *The Wild Seventies*. New York, London, D. Appleton Century Co., Inc., 1941.

Lynn, Kenneth S. *The Dream of Success*. Boston, Little, Brown, 1955.

Madison, Charles A. *American Labor Leaders*. New York, Harper's, 1950.

———. *Critics and Crusaders*. New York, H. Holt & Co., 1947.

Mann, Arthur. *Yankee Reformers in the Urban Age*. Cambridge, Belknap Press of the Harvard University Press, 1954.

Marcosson, Isaac. *David Graham Phillips and His Times*. New York, Dodd Mead & Co., 1932.

Maurice, Arthur B. *New York in Fiction*. New York, Dodd Mead & Co., 1901.

May, Henry F. *The End of American Innocence*. New York, Knopf, 1959.

McCormick, John. *Catastrophe and Imgination*. London, Longmans, Green, 1957.

Merriam, Charles E. *American Political Ideas*. New York, The Macmillan Co., 1923.

Meyer, Karl E. *The New America, Politics and Society in the Age of the Smooth Deal*. New York, Basic Books, Inc., 1961.

Millgate, Martin. *American Social Fiction*. New York, Barnes & Noble, 1964.

Mills, C. Wright. *White Collar*. New York, Oxford University Press, 1951.

Morgan, H. Wayne, ed. *American Socialism, 1900–1960*. Englewood Cliffs, N. J., Prentice–Hall, Inc., 1964.

———. *The Gilded Age: A Reappraisal.* Syracuse, N. Y., Syracuse University Press, 1963.

Morris, Lloyd. *Postscript to Yesterday.* New York, Random House, 1947.

Mowry, George E. *The Era of Theodore Roosevelt, 1900–1912.* New York, Harper & Bros., 1958.

Mumford, Lewis. *The Golden Day.* New York, Boni & Liveright, 1926.

Myers, Gustavus. *History of the Great American Fortunes.* Chicago, C. H. Kerr Co., 1907.

Nugent, Walter T. K. *The Tolerant Populists.* Chicago & London, University of Chicago Press, 1963.

Nye, Russel B. *Midwestern Progressive Politics.* East Lansing, Michigan State University Press, 1959.

Orth, Samuel P. *The Boss and the Machine.* New Haven, Yale University Press, 1920.

Parkes, Henry B. *The American Experience.* New York, Knopf, 1947.

Parrington, V. L. *Main Currents in American Thought.* New York, Harcourt, Brace., 1927.

Parrington, V. L. Jr. *American Dreams.* Providence, R. I., Brown University Studies, 1947.

Pattee, Fred L. *The New American Literature, 1890–1930.* New York, London, The Century Co., 1930.

Pollack, Norman. *The Populist Response to Industrial America.* Cambridge, Harvard University Press, 1962.

Quinn, Arthur H. *American Fiction.* New York, London, D. Appleton Century Co., 1936.

Regier, C. C. *The Era of the Muckrakers.* Chapel Hill, N.C., University of North Carolina Press, 1932.

Rideout, Walter. *The Radical Novel in America.* Cambridge, Harvard University Press, 1956.

Rose, Lisle A. *A Survey of American Economic Fiction, 1902–1909.* Chicago (Part of University of Chicago Thesis,

1935), private edition, distributed by the University of Chicago Libraries, 1938.

Ross, John F. *The Social Criticism of Fenimore Cooper.* Berkeley, Calif., University of California Press, 1933.

Rossiter, Clinton. *The American Presidency.* New York, Harcourt Brace, 1956.

———. *Parties and Politics in America.* Ithaca, New York, Cornell University Press, 1960.

Rubin, Louis D., Jr. *The Faraway Country : Writers of the Modern South.* Seattle, Washington, University of Washington Press, 1963.

Sayre, Robert F. *The Examined Self: Benjamin Franklin, Henry Adams, Henry James.* Princeton, N.J., Princeton University Press, 1964.

Schlesinger, Arthur M. *The American as Reformer.* Cambridge, Harvard University Press, 1950.

———. *Political and Social Growth of the American People.* New York, The Macmillan Co., 1941.

———. *The Rise of the City, 1878–1898.* New York, The Macmillan Co., 1933.

Schorer, Mark. *Sinclair Lewis.* New York, Toronto, London, McGraw-Hill Book Co., Inc., 1961.

Seitz, Don C. *The Dreadful Decade, 1869–1879.* Indianapolis, Indiana, Bobbs Merrill, 1926.

Speare, Morris E. *The Political Novel, Its Development in England and America.* New York, Oxford University Press, 1924.

Spiller, Robert, *et al.,* eds. *Literary History of the United States,* New York, The Macmillan Co., 1948.

Taylor, Walter F. *The Economic Novel in America.* Chapel Hill, N. C., University of North Carolina Press, 1942.

Thorp, Willard. *American Writing in the Twentieth Century.* Cambridge, Harvard University Press, 1960.

Titus, Warren I. *Winston Churchill.* New York, Twayne Publishers, Inc., 1963.

Trilling, Lionel. *The Liberal Imagination*. New York, Viking Press, 1950.

Underwood, John C. *Literature and Insurgency*. New York, M. Kennerly, 1914.

Van Devander, Charles. *The Big Bosses*. New York, Howell Soskin, 1944.

Van Doren, Carl. *Contemporary American Novelists*. New York, The Macmillan Co., 1928.

Wecter, Dixon. *The Age of the Great Depression, 1929–1941*. New York, The Macmillan Co., 1948.

Weinberg, Arthur and Lila Weinberg, eds. *The Muckrakers*. New York, Simon & Schuster, 1961.

Wish, Harvey. *Contemporary America*. New York, Harper & Bros., 1961 (3rd edition).

Wood, James P. *Magazines in the United States*. New York, The Ronald Press, 1949.

Zink, Harold. *City Bosses in the United States*. Durham, N. C., Duke University Press, 1930.

III. Secondary Sources—Articles

Arvin, Newton. "Literature and Social Change," *Modern Quarterly*, Vol. 6 (Summer, 1932), 20–25.

Basso, Hamilton. "The Huey Long Legend," *Life*, Vol. 21, No. 6 (December 9, 1946), 106–21.

Bentwich, Norman. "The Novel as a Political Force," *The Living Age*, Vol. 251 (December 29, 1906), 771–78.

Brooks, Obed. "The Problem of the Social Novel," *Modern Quarterly*, Vol. 6 (Autumn, 1932), 77–82.

Burns, Wayne. "The Novelist as Revolutionary," *Arizona Quarterly*, Vol. 7 (Spring, 1951), 13–27.

Cassady, Edward E. "Muckraking in the Gilded Age," *American Literature*, Vol. 13 (May, 1941), 135–41.

Chamberlain, John. "The Businessman in Fiction," *Fortune*, Vol. 38, No. 2 (November, 1948), 134–48.

Cooper, Frederick T. "Some Representative American Story

Tellers: Winston Churchill," *Bookman*, Vol. 31 (May, 1910), 246–53.

Duffey, Bernard I. "Progressivism and Personal Revolt," *The Centennial Review*, Vol. 2 (Spring, 1958), 125–38.

Fairfield, Roy P. "Benjamin Orange Flower: Father of the Muckrakers," *American Literature*, Vol. 22 (November, 1950), 272–82.

Filler, Louis. "Political Literature: A Post-Mortem," *South West Review*, Vol. 39 (Summer, 1954), 185–93.

———. "The Reputation of David Graham Phillips," *Antioch Review*, Vol. 11 (December, 1951), 475–88.

Fisher, H.A.L. "The Political Novel," *Cornhill Magazine*, n.s., Vol. 64 (January, 1928), 25–38.

Forbes, Allyn B. "The Literary Quest for Utopia, 1880–1900," *Social Forces*, Vol. 6 (December, 1927), 179.

Frohock, Wilbur M. "Mr. Warren's Albatross," *South West Review*, Vol. 36 (Winter, 1951), 48–59.

Glicksberg, Charles I. "Proletarian Fiction in the United States," *Dalhousie Review*, Vol. 17 (April, 1937), 22–32.

Goodwin, George, Jr. "The Last Hurrahs: George Apley & Frank Skeffington," *The Massachusetts Review*, Vol. 1 (Spring, 1960), 461–71.

Harrington, Fred H. "Literary Aspects of American Anti-Imperialism," *New England Quarterly*, Vol. 10 (December, 1937), 650–67.

Hicks, Granville. "Fiction and Social Criticism," *College English*, Vol. 13 (April, 1952), 355–61.

Hofstadter, Richard and Beatrice Hofstadter. "Winston Churchill: A Study in the Popular Novel," *American Quarterly*, Vol. 2 (Spring, 1950), 12–28.

Howe, Irving. "The Political Novel," *Tomorrow*, Vol. 10 (May, 1951), 51–58.

Hynes, Sam. "Robert Penn Warren: The Symbolic Journey," *University of Kansas City Review*, Vol. 17 (Summer, 1951), 279–85.

James, Henry. Review of *Honest John Vane, Nation,* Vol. 19 (December 31, 1874), 441–42.

——. Review of *Playing the Mischief, Nation,* Vol. 21 (August 12, 1875), 106.

Jones, Joseph. "Petroleum V. Nasby Tries the Novel . . . ," *University of Texas Studies in English,* Vol. 30 (1951), 202–18.

Kaplan, Charles. "Jack Burden: Modern Ishmael," *College English,* Vol. 22 (October, 1960), 19–24.

Koenig, Louis W. Review of Blair Bolles' *Men of Good Intentions, Saturday Review,* Vol. 43, No. 3 (August 6, 1960), 22–23.

Kristol, Irving. "Strange Gods on Capitol Hill." Review of Allen Drury's *Advise and Consent, The Reporter,* Vol. 21 (November 12, 1959), 38–40.

Lewis, Wyndham. "The Propagandist in Fiction," *New York Times Current History,* Vol. 40 (August, 1934), 567–72.

McKitrick, Eric L. "The Study of Corruption,'" *Political Science Quarterly,* Vol. 72 (December, 1957), 502–14.

Meyer, Cord, Jr. Review of Allen Drury's *Advise and Consent, The Kenyon Review,* Vol. 22 (Spring, 1960), 327–31.

"Politics or Commitment?" *Times Literary Supplement* (September 1, 1961), 580.

Quinn, Arthur. "American Literature and American Politics," *Proceedings of the American Antiquarian Society,* n. s., Vol. 54 (April 19, 1944), 59–112.

Rahv, Philip. "Proletarian Literature: A Political Autopsy," *Southern Review,* Vol. 4 (Winter, 1939), 616–28.

Rice, Wallace. "In Political Fiction," *The World Today,* Vol. 4 (June, 1903), 726–30.

Rose, Lisle A. "A Bibliographical Survey of Economic and Political Writings, 1865–1900," *American Literature,* Vol. 15 (January, 1944), 381–410.

Rubin, Louis D., Jr. "Politics and the Novel," Address before the American Political Science Association, September 8, 1961.

Sanford, Charles L. "Classics of American Reform Literature," *American Quarterly*, Vol. 10 (Fall, 1958), 295–311.

Shurter, Robert L. "The Utopian Novel in America, 1888–1900," *South Atlantic Quarterly*, Vol. 34 (April, 1935), 137–44.

Strauss, Harold. "Realism in the Proletarian Novel," *Yale Review*, Vol. 28 (Winter, 1939), 360–74.

Williams, Francis C. "The Politician in Fiction," *Bookman*, Vol. 15 (July, 1902), 463–65.

———. "Red Blood in Fiction," *The World's Work*, Vol. 6 (July, 1903), 3694–702.

Yoder, Edwin M., Jr. Review of James Hulbert's *Noon on the Third Day*, *Saturday Review*, Vol. 45, No. 3 (September 8, 1962), 50.

IV. Secondary Sources—Unpublished Dissertations

Baker, Donald G. "Political Values in Popular Fiction, 1919–1959." Syracuse, 1961.

Dickens, William B. "A Guide to the American Political Novel, 1865–1910." Michigan, 1953.

Ferrell, Wilfred A. "Portrait of the Politician in the American Novel: 1870–1910." Texas, n.d.

Johnson, Jean O. "The American Political Novel in the Nineteenth Century." Boston University, 1958.

Lyndenberg, John. "Pre-Muckraking." Harvard, 1946.

Mayberry, George. Industrialism and the Industrial Worker in the American Novel." Harvard, 1942.

Index

Index

Index

The American Political Novel has been cast on the Linotype in eleven-point Electra. Three points of spacing between the lines lend added legibility to a type face acclaimed for its inherent charm of design. The paper on which this book is printed bears the watermark of the University of Oklahoma Press and is designed for an effective life of at least three hundred years.

UNIVERSITY OF OKLAHOMA PRESS
Norman

Gordon

22504

rican political novel

DATE DUE			